Wheeled Vehicles

of the

Wehrmacht

1933–45

Edited by Chris Ellis

AVOCET BOOKS
in association with
KRISTALL PRODUCTIONS

First published in this form 1974
New edition 1988

ISBN 0 904811 12 3

Produced by Kristall Productions Ltd, 71b Maple Road, Surbiton, Surrey KT6 4AG for Avocet Books, 21 Mill Road, Great Gransden, Sandy, Bedfordshire SG19 3AG.

Printed and bound in Great Britain by Adlard & Son Ltd, Letchworth, Herts SG6 1JS.

Introduction

THIS book sets out to provide the military enthusiast with an easy to follow guide to the major types of wheeled motor vehicle used by the Wehrmacht for all transportation purposes in World War 2. While several other books have been published dealing with Wehrmacht vehicles and their history in varying degrees of detail, most of these, though giving quite considerable technical coverage, do so largely from the manufacturers' viewpoint, with emphasis on individual vehicle models and makers' designations. Military designations and uses usually take second place. The German ordnance department issued its own catalogue of vehicle types which gave all essential data about each type. This was the loose-leaf D.600 *Unhaltswerte ber Kraftfahrzeuge und Gerat,* itself quite a collector's piece today. This illustrated each vehicle type rather than make, for the Wehrmacht issued specifications for different classes of vehicle and several makers might supply chassis for any given class or type of vehicle. Official documentation rarely referred to makers in any given designations except where it affected mechanical matters, such as in a user handbook. The D.600 gives a clear picture of the different types of vehicle in service but is difficult for a non-German speaker to work from; fortunately, however, the U.S. Army Ordnance Technical Intelligence Unit in late 1942 produced what amounted to an English translation of the October 1940 edition of D.600, omitting a few types like tracked armoured vehicles. Material from this publication, including the original D.600 illustrations, forms the main basis of this book, but a simple non-technical description of vehicle development is given as well, plus a supplement covering Schell-Programm vehicles and others not in the 1940 edition of D.600. Within the limits of the size of the present volume, as comprehensive coverage as possible has been given and all 'key' types and makes are included. Clearly, however, it would be physically impossible to show every possible combination of chassis/body/type for this would multiply the size of the book, and hence its price, several times. For instance there were over 100 types for the Opel Blitzwagen with the standard box body, most of them as intended replacements for earlier types shown in this book. Here only a couple are shown for all were externally identical except for small detail fittings. Also, for the sake of space, it has not been possible to include prototypes, captured or impressed vehicles, non-standard types made in small runs, and other oddities – this is essentially a guide to standard types on the ordnance inventory with only one or two exceptions. A key to the actual chassis shown with each type (where known) is given on the last page of this book which should be an added aid to identification of vehicles by maker as well as type.

Acknowledgements

FOR assistance in gathering together the material and illustrations used in this book, publisher and editor would like to thank R. P. Hunnicutt, H. L. Doyle, David List, Peter Chamberlain, and the Imperial War Museum, London.

A typical concentration of German wheeled transport waiting to move forward in April 1941 on the day Germany invaded Russi Left foreground is a Kfz 12, an (E) chassis (standard) vehicle, built by Horch, with a Steyr-built Kfz 15 on a (O) chassis behi: it. To the right the leading car is another Horch, with a captured British Morris 4 × 2 8 cwt truck behind it.

Contents

DEVELOPMENT OF WEHRMACHT VEHICLES

1. Cars and Personnel Carriers

IN the 1920s the Reichswehr (the German Army) was limited under the terms of the 1919 Versailles Treaty, both in size and in budget. The modest requirements for personnel-carrying vehicles were largely met by the purchase of commercially-built passenger car chassis. These were fitted with a simple type of open body (kubelsitzer) with folding canvas side screens and a folding canvas roof. By 1930 this type of vehicle had proved its utility and trials were held to determine the best makes to adopt in quantity. To meet military requirements and give limited cross-country ability, larger types were specified with, in most cases, lower axle ratios and improved springs. Daimler-Benz, Adler and Wanderer were considered the best as the result of trials and became major types, though other makes were also taken into service. During the 1930s, this type of vehicle saw wide use and, indeed, became one of the most characteristic of German military vehicles. The type was adapted as a radio car, light gun tractor, artillery survey vehicle, and signal car, additional to its original employment as a light personnel carrier.

With the formation of the Wehrmacht (armed forces) in 1933, following Hitler's rise to power, an attempt was made at rationalisation and cars were classified as follows:

Class		Size
Light	Leichte	Any approved make up to 1500 cc.
Medium	Mittlerer	Any approved make up to 3000 cc.
Heavy	Schwere	Any approved make over 3000 cc.

This led to the eventual designation of the following broad categories of car:

Leichte Personenkraftwagen
(Light Passenger/Personnel car)

Designation	Description
–	Light passenger car (as commercial model)
Kfz 1	Light cross-country personnel carrier
Kfz 2	Light signal communications truck
Kfz 2	Light radio car
Kfz 3	Light survey section car
Kfz 2/40	Small repair vehicle

(Kfz = *Kraftfahrzeug* = *motor vehicle*)

Within these categories were several more specialised adaptations, such as siren, traffic control, and PK (propaganda kompanie) vehicles. Also, as detailed later, the Adler 'Favorit' chassis, one make used for the Kfz 1 type, also formed a basis for the Kfz 13 and Kfz 14 light armoured cars which saw extensive service in the late 1930s and early in World War 2.

Mittlerer Personenkraftwagen
(Medium Passenger/Personnel car)

Designation	Description
–	Medium passenger car (as commercial model)
Kfz 11	Medium cross-country personnel carrier
Kfz 12	Medium cross-country personnel car with towing apparatus (ie, tow-hook)
Kfz 15	Signal communications car (or radio car)
Kfz 16	Medium flash and sound ranging (artillery survey) car
Kfz 17	Telephone exchange car (or radio car with van body)
Kfz 18	Emergency repair car or weapons carrier

Schwerer Personenkraftwagen
(Heavy Passenger/Personnel car)

Designation	Description
–	Heavy passenger car (as commercial model)
Kfz 21	Heavy cross-country personnel car

All the foregoing vehicles, being built on commercially available chassis, were designated with the suffix (o) (= handelsublich), indicating the commercial nature of the chassis.

The full designation of a military vehicle in German was long and unwieldy for the non-German speaker, but was precise in its description. Thus the well-known Kfz 1 (its ordnance department designation) was known fully in German as the 'Leichter gelandegangiger Personenkraftwagen (Kfz 1) mit Fahrgestell des leichter Personenkraftwagen (o)'.

Translated into English, this becomes:
'Light cross-country personnel carrier (motor vehicle No. 1) with special chassis for light passenger car (on commercial vehicle chassis)'.

It is interesting to note that in all the English equivalents given in this book, the original translations give the second 'Pkw' in the German designation as 'armoured car' rather than 'passenger car', perhaps some indication of how cumbersome the original designation could be.

In practice, however, the full German description and designation was abbreviated to 'l.gl. Pkw(Kfz 1)' in the case of the example quoted, though there were variations, even in official documentation, in the extent and writing out of the abbreviated form. The 'light passenger car' part of the designation in the quoted example refers to the fact that in the case of this particular vehicle the chassis was that used for the basic civilian model sedan. In the reference pages of this book the original German designation is given together with a common form of abbreviation.

LEFT: Kfz 11 vehicles of a motorised column take advantage of a roadside stream for cleaning up. The doors have been removed from the nearest vehicle and placed across the rear seats. Note the padded leather radiator cover and the wire frame on the nearside wing of foreground vehicle which was fitted for the display of a command flag when required.

BELOW: Nachrichtenkraftwagen (Kfz 15) mit Fahrgestell des mittlerer Pkw (o) was typical of the medium class cars on the commercially-based (o) chassis. Vehicle in this drawing from orginal handbook is the Horch model 8 30.

From the foregoing it can be seen that the chassis and purpose were the governing factors influencing the designation, and the make or manufacturer of the vehicle was considered incidental in official documentation. Thus Adler, Auto-Union, Daimler-Benz, Wanderer, BMW, and Hanomag, all supplied chassis for the Kfz 1 role. Broadly speaking these were similar looking cars, though such parts such as radiators, engines, hoods, and wheelhubs, trademarks, etc, clearly identified the actual makes. Examination of official documents shows that identification of a vehicle by maker appears to have been restricted mainly to user handbooks or maintenance inventories where it was clearly necessary for a particular chassis to be identified. When the maker was identified it was normally as a suffix at the end of the description. In the example previously given this would be expressed as:

'Leichter gelandegangiger Personenkraftwagen (Kfz 1) mit Fahrgestell des leichter Pkw(o) Adler'.

The heavy passenger car chassis class did not enter the ordnance inventory until the middle 1930s and the cars in this class saw only limited service in the late 1930s, thus accounting for the short listing given above.

Einheits Personenkraftwagen

As part of the Wehrmacht's rearmament programme it was decided in 1934 to replace the existing commercially-based chassis with a new range of standardised purpose-built chassis.

It was proposed that the three classes should have many components in common, including suspension units, and that standardised engines would be produced. The light and heavy classes were to have steerable wheels at the back as well as the front, and all would be four-wheel drive. In the event this proved over-ambitious. The first vehicles in the three classes appeared in 1937 – 38 and normal commercial engines were fitted due to the time and expense which would have been needed for the standardised engine programme. Only the early vehicles had rear wheel steering and this feature was dropped in 1939 to simplify production.

Hanomag, Stoewer, and BMW all built light passenger car chassis under the Einheits programme and ordnance designations corresponded to those existing for the

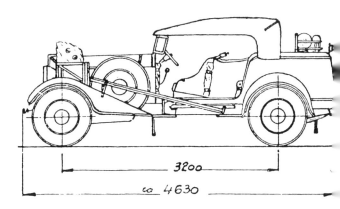

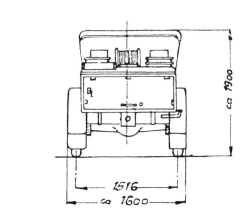

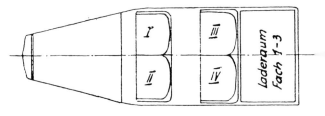

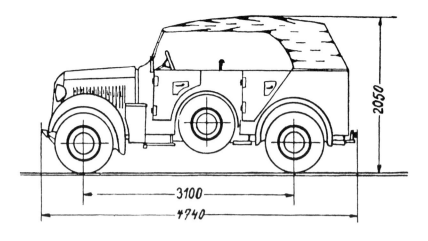 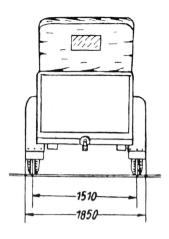

commercial chassis vehicles, except that a Kfz 4 light AA
vehicle with twin MG 34 machine-guns was added to the
range of light types. The full designation of the new
standard vehicles indicated that they were of standardised
rather than commercial derivation. Thus the Kfz 1 was
designated in full:
'Leichter gelandegangiger Personenkraftwagen (Kfz 1)
mit Einheitsfahrgestell 1 fur leichter Pkw'.
In English this roughly translated as:
'Light cross-country personnel carrier (or car) on
standard chassis No. 1 for light passenger car'.
Horch (Auto-Union) built the Einheits programme
vehicles in the medium chassis class and these (E) series
vehicles had designations (Kfz 11 through Kfz 18)
corresponding to (o) series. Radio cars (Kfz 17, etc) in the
medium (E) series had wood hardtops which gave a van-
like appearance to the vehicle.
Horch (Auto-Union) were also the main builders of
Einheits programme heavy chassis cars. The category
came into service later than the other two classes since the
first production chassis, which had rear engines, was used
entirely for armoured car production – the Sd kfz 221,
22, 223, etc, all illustrated in this book. The front engine
Einheits chassis was used for heavy passenger car

BELOW: Daimler-Benz were not
involved in the supply of medium class
passenger cars of Einheits (E) type to the
Wehrmacht. Nonetheless, the firm
produced a vehicle which was virtually to
the same specification, the Mercedes-Benz
5, and over 300 were sold commercially,
mainly for estates and forestry services.
When war came, some saw army service.
This view shows well the rear wheel
steering originally specified for the Einheits
series cars.

*ABOVE: Nachrichtenkraftwagen
(Kfz 15) mit Einheitsfahrgestell fur
mittlerer Personenkraftwagen. Vehicle
depicted is on the Horch model 40 chassis
and shows a typical medium class car on
a Einheits (E) chassis for comparison with
the same class of vehicle on the (o) chassis
as shown on opposite page. BELOW:
TOP TO BOTTOM: Standard chassis
for light, medium, and heavy passenger car
classes in the Einheits (E) range.*

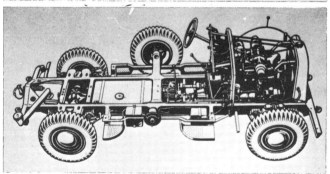

production, the earliest type only having rear wheel steering. In addition to the original Kfz 21 (personnel carrier) category already extant with (o) series vehicles, the new (E) series vehicles were adapted for many new roles. These included the following:

Designation	Description
Kfz 23	Telephone truck
Kfz 83	Light searchlight truck
Kfz 31	Ambulance
Kfz 69	Limber truck (tractor or munition carrier)
Kfz 70	Reconnaissance car
Kfz 81	AA unit light car

All except very early series (E) series vehicles in all classes had metal detachable side doors rather than canvas side screens. The spare wheels were carried externally on the sides in the original design, recessed into the body, but later production vehicles had a wider body (with slightly increased seating capacity) and the spare wheels were then carried inside the body. A few (E) series cars in all classes were given civilian type tourer/convertible bodies to serve as personal transports (kommandeurwagen) for high ranking officers.

ABOVE: This 'clip-on' kit was produce enabling the ordinary medium passenge car to be converted to an 'ersatz' Funk kraftwagen (Kfz 15). The original trun lid was removed and the transmitter receiver controls fitted behind the front sea and can be seen here.

In addition to appearing on the (E) series chassis th standard personnel carrier body was fitted to sever types of commercial, impressed, or captured chassis either indigenous or foreign origin. Among chassis s fitted were Tatra, Adler, Chevrolet, and various othe including captured British 8 cwt trucks.

The (E) series cars had a relatively short productic life, being discontinued from 1941–42 when a ne attempt at rationalisation was introduced as part of th so-called Schell-Programm.

Schell-Programm developments

In 1938 General Schell, Director of Motorisation for th Wehrmacht, introduced a far-sighted plan to cut back c the numerous different makes of (o) type commerciall based vehicles in service. For instance there were over ! different types of car chassis alone and the variety cause huge maintenance and spares supply problems. Th

BELOW: One of the rarer types of car in military service was the Mercedes-Benz G4, a 6 × 4 heavy passenger car, used mainly by high ranking NSDAP leaders (including Hitler himself). Here three cars of this type can be seen, belonging to the formation HQ of the SS-VT unit 'Leibstandarte Adolf Hitler' during the invasion of Poland, September 1939. Armoured car in foreground is a Sd Kfz 221.

ABOVE: *Homely scene in the Western Desert shows a Kfz 15 (Horch model 40) of a battalion HQ in the summer of 1941. Trucks in background are wrecked British vehicles. Note stowage box on wing of car.*

chell-Programm proposed to cut back procurement of ehicles to all types to just a few standard chassis which, a turn, were suitable for both military and commercial ervice. Subsequent events, when production facilities nd material supplies became scarce, more than justified e implementation of the Schell-Programm.

Within the programme itself passenger cars were the st to be affected in terms of production schedules and it as not until 1941 that the Einheits (E) series models ere phased out of manufacture. All of them were nsidered too costly and too complicated for wartime roduction conditions. As the standard light passenger r a new design was chosen, the Volkswagen Typ 82 hich has since become familiarly known as the VW ubelwagen and is one of the best-known vehicles to me out of World War 2. The Volkswagen had been signed in the late 1930s by Dr Ferdinand Porsche as a ar-engined 'people's car' for production in sedan form. 'ith war looming, Porsche was asked to produce a ilitary version, providing a raised suspension, lower ive ratio, and (later) an increased engine capacity. arly tests in the winter of 1939-40 showed the vehicle to extremely handy with a performance nearly matching four-wheel drive vehicle. Put into production in early

1940, the Volkswagen Kubelwagen was completely ubiquitous and its roles included personnel carrier, munition carrier, fuel carrier, ambulance, and engineer vehicle. The body was extremely simple in construction, being of all flat panels. The vehicle weighed only ½ ton (1,000 pounds approx) and could be righted, if overturned, by only two people. Over 52,000 VWs were built by 1945. A companion vehicle was the Volkswagen Typ 166, an amphibious derivative of the Typ 82. Some 14,000 were built, but the Schwimmwagen, as it was called, was too complicated and expensive to build and was discontinued in 1944.

No medium car replacement was included in the Schell-Programm and the heavy car replacement shared the new standard light truck chassis and is described in the next section.

ELOW: Chassis of the military version of the Volkswagen (Typ), which became the standard replacement for the previous types light and medium car chassis. Note the essential simplicity mpared to the Einheits chassis shown on page 7.

2. Trucks

FOR general transport purposes the Reichswehr originally purchased any suitable commercial trucks, but from 1929 more rigid requirements were laid down, and trucks came to be classified as follows:

Class		Size
Light	Leichte	Any approved make with useful load up to 2 tons
Medium	Mittlerer	Any approved make with useful load above 2 tons and up to 3.5 tons
Schwere	Heavy	Any approved make with a useful load over 3.5 tons

Light class

In the light class such commercial 4 × 2 types as Phanomen-Granit, Borgward, and Adler were purchased and were widely used, the first-named make being specially numerous. Ambulance, radio van, and even Kubelsitzer bodies weere fitted to the Phanomen-Granit chassis. To meet military requirements more adequately, a 6 × 4 chassis specification was drawn up by the army in 1929 and several manufacturers produced designs which conformed. The Mercedes-Benz model G3a, Magirus M206, and Bussing-NAG G31 were all built and supplied in the 1930s and fulfilled a number of specialist roles, most of them being illustrated in this book. As with passenger cars the ordnance designation was concerned solely with the vehicle's purpose and no distinction was made of the chassis manufacturer. To take a graphic example, the three sets of scale drawings here (taken from original user handbooks) show a typical case – the Kfz 61, Leichter Fernsprechbetriebskraftwagen auf 1½ T (telephone generator truck on 1½ ton chassis). The drawings show this vehicle's appearance based respectively on each chassis in turn, the van body being common except where dimensional changes were made to fit it to a specific chassis. In the reference section of this book where Kfz 61 vehicles are shown it will be noted that the chassis can be any of the three makes shown here; the drawings should, also be of assistance to readers wishing to identify the chassis make in any of the light truck 6 × 4 variants illustrated in this book.

Best-known of all the 6 × 4 chassis built, and quite distinctive in appearance, was the Krupp model L2H 43 (and its almost identical successor in production, the L2H 143). Popularly known as the Boxer, this chassis had an air-cooled flat-4 square engine (hence its name) with a distinctive sloped hood, an open cab with folding canvas top, and independent rear suspension. The chassis was quite ubiquitous in application and Boxers were seen in a vast number of roles from personnel carrier to gun tractor; most are illustrated in this book. There was also an armoured version, Sd Kfz 247.

The Bussing-NAG, Mercedes, and Daimler-Benz 6 × 4 chassis also formed the basis for the Sd Kfz 231 (6 rad

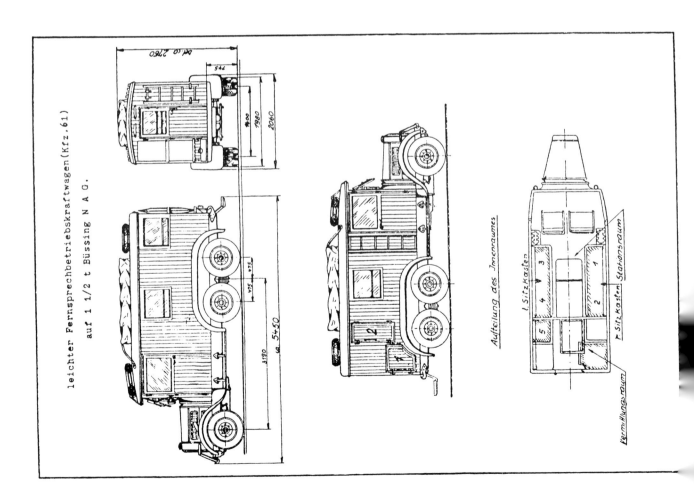

10

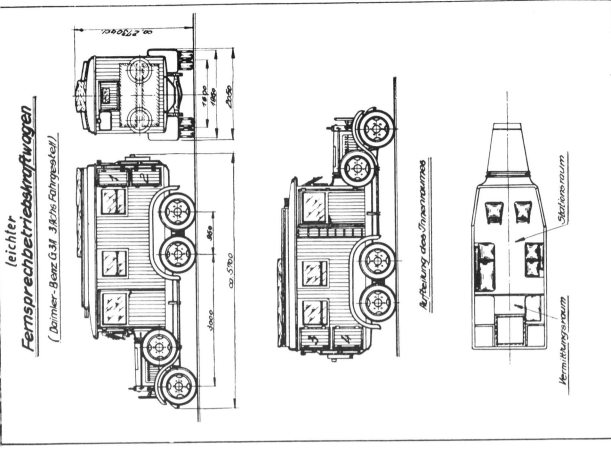

leichter
Fernsprechbetriebskraftwagen
(Daimler-Benz G31 3 Achs-Fahrgestell)

Aufteilung des Innenraumes

Stationsraum

Vermittlungsraum

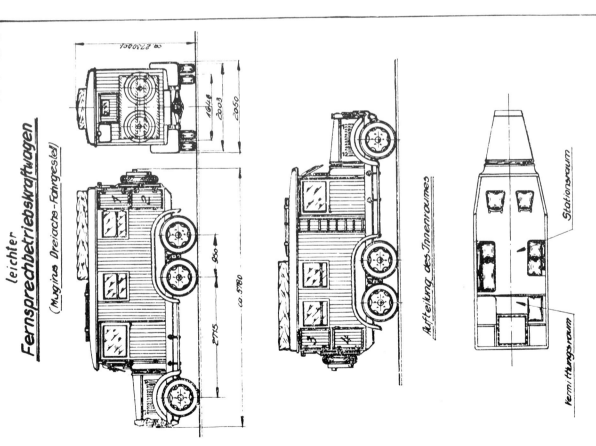

leichter
Fernsprechbetriebskraftwagen
(Magirus Dreiachs-Fahrgestell)

Aufteilung des Innenraumes

Stationsraum

Vermittlungsraum

These three sets of drawings, taken from original user handbooks, give a good comparison of dimensions and appearance between the three main Einheits (E) chassis in the light truck class; Bussing-NAG G31, Magirus M206, Daimler-Benz G3A.

11

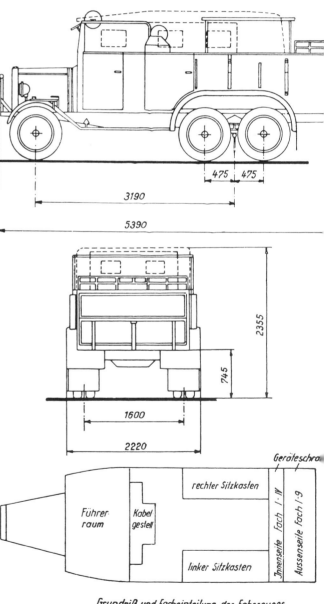

RIGHT: The Krupp model L2H 143 'Boxer' chassis was used for numerous roles. One of its later uses was as the basis of the Fernsprechbetriebskraftwagen (Kfz 19) (= telephone generator truck). Note the distinctive sloped hood.

BELOW, RIGHT: Typical light class 6 × 4 vehicle, in this case the Magirus M206 chassis with body for the Kfz 77 (telephone truck) role.

FOOT OF PAGE: Typical chassis for 1.5 ton Typ-A chassis, in this case for a Steyr 1500A. For typical vehicle on this chassis, see page 124.

armoured car and its derivatives, these being illustrated in this book.

All these six-wheel 'light' Einheits trucks were in production in the 1934–38 period, after which Schell-Programm vehicles replaced them.

Even before the Schell-Programm was introduced the Waffenamt (ordnance department) had produced a design for a 6 × 6 'light' chassis which was intended as a standardised (E) design to replace the various (o) chassis vehicles in the 6 × 4 category. Called the Einheitsdiesel (= standard diesel) it was built by Bussing-NAG, MAN, Daimler-Benz, and Borgward and began replacing the (o) chassis vehicles on the production lines in 1937, production continuing until well into 1940 when Schell-Programm vehicles replaced it.

Schell-Programm developments

In the light truck class a standard type of chassis with a payload of 1.5 tons was proposed. Usually designated '1500' by builders, the chassis was produced in two forms. With conventional 4 × 2 layout it was known as Typ-S (S = standard) which was also known as Wirtschaftstyp (= commercial type). Though suitable for commercial use, the Typ-S also saw extensive military service, specially in secondary supply carrying roles. The specific military version of the same chassis was known as Typ-A (A = allradantrieb = all wheel drive) and was of 4 × 4 layout. Aside from the changes necessitated by the live front axle and different gears, etc, the A and S type were mechanically and structurally similar in all respects. Main producers of 1.5 tons vehicles in the Schell-Programm were Steyr (1500A and 1500 S), Mercedes-Benz (L1500A and L1500S), and Phanomen-Granit (1500A and 1500S models). The latter vehicles were mainly supplied for the ambulance or van role. As part of the Schell-Programm, standard body types were also built and these could be fitted to all chassis in the load class. The van body was used for ambulances, signal trucks, machinery trucks, etc, and was known as a Einheitskastenaufbau (= standard house body).

The light truck chassis was also used as the Schell-Programm replacement for the heavy passenger car and a tourer type body was fitted for command cars (Kommandeurwagen) and a personnel carrier body for other roles (Mannschaftwagen).

Leichter Fernsprechbaukraftwagen (Kfz 77

3190

475 475

5390

2355

745

1600

2220

Geräteschra

Führer raum

Kabel gestell

rechter Sitzkasten

linker Sitzkasten

Innenseite Fach I · IV

Aussenseite Fach I·9

Grundriß und Facheinteilung des Fahrzeuges.

Medium class

[D]evelopment of medium class trucks – with a payload of [2] tons cross-country and 3 tons on the road – was [p]arallel to light class vehicles. Chassis and layout was [si]milar but bigger. Major vehicles involved were the [K]rupp L3H 63 and its similar successor, the L3H 163, [th]e Henschel 33B1 and its successors the 33D1 and 33 G1 [(g]asoline and diesel models respectively), the Daimler-[B]enz LG3000, and the Bussing-NAG III GL6. As before [th]e chassis were used for numerous roles, typical being [th]e Kfz 72 printing vehicle (in several forms), the Kfz 354 [ph]otographic truck, and the Pioneerkraftwagen I [en]gineers' truck). Of these chassis the Henschel was the [m]ost numerous, Magirus also building this vehicle under [li]cence from 1938 on. These different vehicles were [v]ariously in production in the 1930–38 period, but the [H]enschel was built until 1940.

Schell-Programm developments

[F]or the medium load class, a 3 ton rating was specified [in] the Schell-Programm. As with the light trucks, A (4 × [4)] and S (4 × 2) type chassis were built, the most usual [m]anufacturer's model designation being 3000A or [3]000S. Major builder of these vehicles was Opel, whose [4]× 2 and 4 × 4 models were probably the best-known [of] all wartime German trucks. The Blitzwagen was the [n]ame given to the model 6700A 4 × 4 version while type [3]-36 was the maker's own designation for the original 4 [×]2 model. In 1944 Daimler-Benz started to build the [sa]me vehicle under licence. Previously Daimler-Benz had [b]uilt their own Schell-Programm design, the L3000A and [L]3000S. Magirus and Borgward also built 3 ton class [ve]hicles in S and A forms while Ford built S type only. [T]here were over 100 official types of body (many [va]riatons on the standard house type) which could be [fit]ted to 3 ton class chassis. A long wheelbase version of [th]e chassis was also produced, mainly for use with a bus [b]ody (Wehrmachtbus) which in turn could be adapted [in]ternally as a personnel carrier, an ambulance, signals [ve]hicle, or command vehicle.

In 1944 shortage of steel forced the introduction of a [ne]w simple utility cab made of pressed cardboard over a [tim]ber framework – this 'ersatz' cab was known as a [W]ehrmacht-Einheitsfahrerhaus. It was dimensioned and [de]signed so that it would fit all weight classes of Schell-[Pr]ogramm chassis.

Another innovation was the Maultier - a semi-tracked [ve]rsion of the standard truck. This was evolved on the [Ea]stern Front to produce a load carrier with improved [tra]ction in conditions of extensive snow, ice, and mud [wh]ere even four-wheel drive vehicles found the going [ve]ry difficult. Carden-Loyd type track units with tracks [of] the PzKpfw I type were fitted in place of the rear [wh]eels, the back axle being moved forward while the

BELOW: Chassis of the Einheitsdiesell standard light truck.

Schwerer Fernsprechkraftwagen
(m. gl. Lkw. off. (o)).

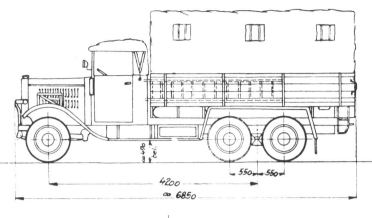

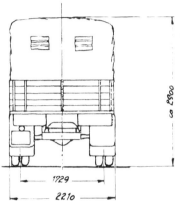

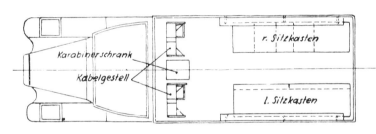

Grundriß und Facheinteilung des Fahrzeugs.

ABOVE: Bussing-NAG III GL6 was typical of 6 × 4 medium class trucks. Here it forms the basis for a heavy telephone truck.

drive shaft was shortened. The chassis was strengthened and brake levers for the track units were added in the cab to operate the original rear wheel brake drums and so assist in steering by means of track-braking. The rating on Maultiers was reduced to 2 tons.

The 3 ton class vehicles of the Schell-Programm the most numerous built and they remained in production throughout World War 2 and for several years afterwards.

Heavy class

In pre-war years heavy trucks purchased by the Wehrmacht were restricted to conventional commercial types. These were supplemented in the 1939-40 period by a few heavy military trucks of Austrian, Czech, or French origin acquired as a result of occupation of the countries concerned.

Schell-Programm developments

Standard military heavy class trucks resulted entirely from the Schell-Programm. This specified 4.5 tons as the payload rating. Bussing-NAG (4500A and 4500S), MAN, and Daimler-Benz (L4500A and L4500S) were major manufacturers in the 1941–45 period and nearly 42,000 vehicles in this class were built, latterly with the ersatz cab.

The final heavy truck class allowed for in the Schell-Programm was 6.5 tons. The Czech firm of Tatra was the sole producer of this size of vehicle in the Schell-Programm, a 6 × 6 diesel V-12 engined model entering production in 1943. Relatively few were built at this late stage of the war. There was also an externally similar 8 ton version (model 8000A) produced just before the end of the war.

3. Other Vehicles

Motor Cycles

In pre-war days the Wehrmacht used a vast number of different makes of motor cycle, both solo machines and combinations. There were over 100 different types on the inventory in 1938–39. The Schell-Programm greatly reduced this proliferation. During World War 2 the heavy 750 cc machine with shaft-drive to the side-car wheel (3 × 2) was the most numerous type. Built by BMW (R75) and Zundapp (KS750), this outfit could carry a MG 34 machine gun on the side-car and was used by all arms. Reconnaissance units used these heavy motor cycle combinations extensively in the early part of the war. Latterly light cars took over most of the recce and liaison roles originally given to motor cycles, which were not tough enough, for example, for conditions on the Eastern Front.

In 1944, production of the heavy 750 cc units ceased and all of previous motor cycle types in service only the DRW RT125 and NZ350 (both dating from 1938–39) remained in production, these being adequate for despatch rider duties. There were several other major makes of motor cycle in German military service, including such types as the BMW R12 and NSU 2500S, but space allows only the first four models mentioned to be illustrated in this book.

An unusual vehicle, virtually a half-track motor cycle, was the NSU Kettenrad, which was officially classed as a light tractor. It had a motor cycle front end with a twin track unit and passenger/cargo section at the rear. This vehicle was originally developed as equipment for the airborne forces, being the largest tractor which could be carried inside (or slung beneath) the Junkers Ju 52 transport aircraft. First used in 1941 during the airborne assault on Crete, the Kettenrad was later used also by army units, particularly on the Eastern Front.

RIGHT, TOP TO BOTTOM: Schell-Programm trucks: Opel model 3.6-36S (4 × 2) Typ-S 3 ton class. Opel model 6700A Typ-A (4 × 4), 3 ton class. Typical Typ-A 3 ton class chassis, this for the Mercedes-Benz Model L3000A. Typical Maultier half-track conversion, this one on a Ford Model V 3000S chassis. Typical Maultier chassis, this one for a Maultier conversion on the Klockner-Humboldt-Deutz Model S3000.

Tractors

Conditions on the Eastern front where roads already poor were turned to seas of mud or slush in winter, dictated the development of the Raupenschlepper-Ost (tracked tractor-east) as a load carrier and towing vehicle. Built by Steyr, the original model (RSO/O1) had a commercial type pressed steel truck cab and wood cargo body. The major production model, however (RSO/O3) had a much simplified cab with flat panels and folding canvas top. These RSOs proved very useful and some were later used on the Western front in 1945. Though not wheeled in the sense of a truck, these vehicles are included in this book since they were mainly intended to fulfil the role of a truck. Czech-built Praga tractors, also included in this book, saw quite extensive service mainly for towing artillery or carrying ammunition. Major wheeled artillery tractors were the Hanomag SS100 Schwerer Radschlepper (shown on this page) and a very similar Faun vehicle. A heavy 6 × 6 tractor built by Kaeble saw limited service to tow heavy trailers and ordnance. For service in Russia the Ostradschlepper (east wheeled tractor) was produced, with large spudded wheels and conventional truck cab and body. These vehicles were built by Skoda.

TOP: Typical 4½ ton class truck from the Schell-Programm. This is the Bussing-NAG Model 4.500S (Typ-S, 4 × 2). ABOVE: Typical 4½ ton chassis from the Schell-Programm. This is the Mercedes-Benz Model L4500S (Typ-S, 4 × 2).

BELOW: Rear view and chassis of the Hanomag 100 HP heavy road tractor – Schwerer Radschlepper (o). See also page 73.

Trailers

A big selection of trailers is shown in this book, most of them having a clearly defined function. It is worth pointing out that the various Sonderhangen (special trailers) shown were considered to be transport items, not part of the artillery equipment (e.g. Flak 36) to which they were normally fitted.

Late in the war the appearance of very heavy tanks necessitated the procurement of heavy commercial trailers and examples of these are shown. Even these were too narrow to carry a Tiger or King Tiger tank properly and the tracks of these vehicles overhung the trailer sides.

Some wheeled vehicles were converted to carry AA guns; a number of Leichter Flakkraftwagen (Kfz 81), normally used as tractors for light AA guns (see page 40), were modified to carry a 2 cm Flak 30 mount in the rear compartment. Note masked headlamps on this Luftwaffe example (IWM-M20384).

WEHRMACHT STANDARD VEHICLES

RIGHT: On the outbreak of war many civilian vehicles of suitable type were taken into Wehrmacht service. Classified as a Mittlerer Personenkraftwagen (o) is this Horch tourer, used as a general's staff car in 1940. It carries command pennants, a civil licence plate, and a 'WH' sign indicating its military role.

LIGHT PASSENGER CAR
. Pkw. (o)

Net weight	1,100 kg	2,425 lb.
Pay load	400 kg	882 lb.
Gross weight	1,500 kg	3,307 lb.
Weight: Front axle	625 kg	1,378 lb.
Weight: Rear axle	875 kg	1,929 lb.
Length (overall)	4,100 mm	13 ft., 5 ins.
Width (overall)	1,500 mm	4 ft., 11 ins.
Height (overall)	1,600 mm	5 ft., 3 ins.
Ground clearance	180 mm	7 ins.
Tread centers	1,200 mm	47 ins.
Wheelbase	2,600 mm	102 ins.
Wheel width	125 mm	4⅞ ins.
Angle of approach		50°
Angle of departure		20°
Seating capacity		1–3
Fording depth	400 mm	15¾ ins.
Climbing ability		17°
Overturn gradient (lengthwise)		60°
Overturn gradient (crosswise)		20°
Turning radius	11 meters	36 ft., 1 in.
Trailer load		
Engine horsepower	37 c–v	36.5 hp
Piston displacement	1,500 cu cm	90 cu. ins.
Fuel tank capacity	35 liters	9¼ gal.
Highway fuel consumption		23.5 m.p.g.

German nomenclature: leichter Personenkraftwagen (o).

English designation: Light passenger car (standard commercial vehicle).

LIGHT CROSS-COUNTRY PERSONNEL CARRIER
. gl. Pkw. (Kfz. 1)

Net weight	1,000 kg	2,204 lb.
Pay load	300 kg	661 lb.
Gross weight	1,300 kg	2,865 lb.
Weight: Front axle	560 kg	1,234 lb.
Weight: Rear axle	740 kg	1,631 lb.
Length (overall)	4,100 mm	13 ft., 5 ins.
Width (overall)	1,500 mm	4 ft., 11 ins.
Height (overall)	1,600 mm	5 ft., 3 ins.
Ground clearance	180 mm	7 ins.
Tread centers	1,200 mm	47 ins.
Wheelbase	2,600 mm	102 ins.
Wheel width	125 mm	4⅞ ins.
Angle of approach		60°
Angle of departure		30°
Seating capacity		3
Fording depth	500 mm	19¾ ins.
Climbing ability		14°–16°
Overturn gradient (lengthwise)		50°
Overturn gradient (crosswise)		40°
Turning radius	11 meters	36 ft., 1 in.
Trailer load		
Engine horsepower	40 c–v	39.44 hp
Piston displacement	1,500 cu cm	90 cu. ins.
Fuel tank capacity	40 liters	10.6 gal.
Highway fuel consumption		23.5 m.p.g.
Average terrain fuel consumption		15.7 m.p.g.

German nomenclature: leichter geländegängiger Personenkraftwagen (Kfz. 1) mit Fahrgestell des leichter Pkw. (o).

English designation: Light cross-country personnel carrier with special chassis for light armored car (standard commercial vehicle).

LIGHT CROSS-COUNTRY PERSONNEL CARRIER
l. gl. Pkw. (Kfz. 1)

German nomenclature: leichter geländegängiger Personenkraftwagen (Kfz. 1) mit Einheitsfahrgestell I für leichter Pkw.

English designation: Light cross-country personnel carrier with standard chassis I for light armored car.

Net weight	1,700 kg	3,748 lb.
Pay load	500 kg	1,102 lb.
Gross weight	2,200 kg	4,850 lb.
Weight: Front axle	1,050 kg	2,315 lb.
Weight: Rear axle	1,150 kg	2,525 lb.
Length (overall)	3,850 mm	12 ft., 7 ins.
Width (overall)	1,690 mm	5 ft., 6 ins.
Height (overall)	1,900 mm	6 ft., 3 ins.
Ground clearance	235 mm	9¼ ins.
Tread centers	1,400 mm	4 ft., 7 ins.
Wheelbase	2,400 mm	94 ins.
Wheel width	158 mm	6¼ ins.
Angle of approach		60°
Angle of departure		45°
Seating capacity		3
Fording depth	500 mm	19¾ ins.
Climbing ability		30°
Overturn gradient (lengthwise)		40°
Overturn gradient (crosswise)		30°
Turning radius	12/6.5 meters	39 ft., 4 ins./ ft., 4 ins.
Trailer load		
Engine horsepower	45 c—v	44.3 hp
Piston displacement	2,000 cu cm	120 cu. ins.
Fuel tank capacity	60 liters	15.9 gal.
Highway fuel consumption		13.6 m.p.g.
Average terrain fuel consumption		9.4 m.p.g.

SIGNAL COMMUNICATIONS TRUCK
Nachr. Kw. (Kfz. 2)

German nomenclature: Nachrichtenkraftwagen (Kfz. 2) mit Fahrgestell des leichter Pkw. (o).

English designation: Signal communications truck or signal service reconnaissance car with special chassis I for light armored car (standard commercial vehicle).

Net weight	1,000 kg	2,204 lb.
Pay load	300 kg	664 lb.
Gross weight	1,300 kg	2,865 lb.
Weight: Front axle	560 kg	1,234 lb.
Weight: Rear axle	740 kg	1,631 lb.
Length (overall)	4,100 mm	13 ft., 5 ins.
Width (overall)	1,500 mm	4 ft., 11 ins.
Height (overall)	1,600 mm	5 ft., 3 ins.
Ground clearance	190 mm	7½ ins.
Tread centers	1,200 mm	3 ft., 11 ins.
Wheelbase	2,600 mm	102 ins.
Wheel width	125 mm	4⅞ ins.
Angle of approach		70°
Angle of departure		1
Seating capacity		30°
Fording depth	500 mm	19¾ ins.
Climbing ability		16°
Overturn gradient (lengthwise)		50°
Overturn gradient (crosswise)		20°
Turning radius	11 meters	36 ft., 1 in.
Trailer load		
Engine horsepower	30 c—v	29.5 hp
Piston displacement	1,500 cu cm	90 cu. ins.
Fuel tank capacity	30 liters	7.9 gal.
Highway fuel consumption		23.5 m.p.g.
Average terrain fuel consumption		15.7 m.p.g.

COMMUNICATIONS CAR
Nachr. Kw. (Kfz. 2)

German nomenclature: Nachrichtenkraftwagen (Kfz. 2) mit Einheitsfahrgestell I für leichter Pkw.

English designation: Communications car with standard chassis I for light armored car.

Net weight	1,700 kg	3,748 lb.
Pay load	500 kg	1,102 lb.
Gross weight	2,200 kg	4,850 lb.
Weight: Front axle	1,000 kg	2,204 lb.
Weight: Rear axle	1,200 kg	2,645 lb.
Length (overall)	3,850 mm	12 ft., 7 ins.
Width (overall)	1,700 mm	5 ft., 11 ins.
Height (overall)	1,900 mm	6 ft., 3 ins.
Ground clearance	235 mm	9¼ ins.
Tread centers	1,400 mm	4 ft., 7 ins.
Wheelbase	2,400 mm	94 ins.
Wheel width	158 mm	6¼ ins.
Angle of approach		60°
Angle of departure		45°
Seating capacity		2
Fording depth	500 mm	19¾ ins.
Climbing ability		30°
Overturn gradient (lengthwise)		50°
Overturn gradient (crosswise)		30°
Turning radius	12/6.5 meters	39 ft., 4 ins./2 ft., 4 ins.
Trailer load		
Engine horsepower	45 c-v	44.4 hp
Piston displacement	2000 cu cm	120 cu. ins.
Fuel tank capacity	60 liters	15.9 gal.
Highway fuel consumption		13.6 m.p.g.
Average terrain fuel consumption		9.4 m.p.g.

SIGNAL COMMUNICATIONS TRUCK
Nachr. Kw. (Kfz. 2)

German nomenclature: Nachrichtenkraftwagen (Kfz. 2) mit Fahrgestell des mittleren Pkw. (o).

English designation: Signal communications truck with special chassis for medium armored car (standard commercial vehicle).

Net weight	1,200 kg	2,645 lb.
Pay load	500 kg	1,102 lb.
Gross weight	1,700 kg	3,747 lb.
Weight: Front axle	820 kg	1,808 lb.
Weight: Rear axle	880 kg	1,940 lb.
Length (overall)	4,100 mm	13 ft., 5 ins.
Width (overall)	1,580 mm	5 ft., 2 ins.
Height (overall)	1,800 mm	5 ft., 11 ins.
Ground clearance	220 mm	8⅝ ins.
Tread centers	1,350 mm	4 ft., 5 ins.
Wheelbase	2,300 mm	90 ins.
Wheel width	160 mm	6¼ ins.
Angle of approach		50°
Angle of departure		30°
Seating capacity		2
Fording depth	400 mm	15¾ ins.
Climbing ability		17°
Overturn gradient (lengthwise)		45°
Overturn gradient (crosswise)		30°
Turning radius	12 meters	39 ft., 4 ins.
Trailer load		
Engine horsepower	45 c-v	44.4 hp
Piston displacement	2,000 cu cm	120 cu. ins.
Fuel tank capacity	60 liters	15.9 gal.
Highway fuel consumption		18.1 m.p.g.
Average terrain fuel consumption		9.8 m.p.g.

MOBILE SIREN
K. Si.

German nomenclature: Kraftfahrsirene (leichter geländegängiger Pkw.) (o).

English designation: Mobile siren (light cross-country
personnel carrier), (standard commercial vehicle).

Net weight	930 kg	2,050 lb.
Pay load	435 kg	958 lb.
Gross weight	1,365 kg	3,008 lb.
Weight: Front axle	585 kg	1,289 lb.
Weight: Rear axle	780 kg	1,719 lb.
Length (overall)	4,100 mm	13 ft., 5 ins.
Width (overall)	1,500 mm	4 ft., 11 ins.
Height (overall)	2,700 mm	8 ft., 10 ins.
Ground clearance	180 mm	7 1/8 ins.
Tread centers	1,200 mm	3 ft., 11 ins.
Wheelbase	2,460 mm	97 ins.
Wheel width	125 mm	4 7/8 ins.
Angle of approach		60°
Angle of departure		30°
Seating capacity		3
Fording depth	500 mm	19 7/8 ins.
Climbing ability		16°
Overturn gradient (lengthwise)		50°
Overturn gradient (crosswise)		40°
Turning radius	12.8 meters	42 ft.
Trailer load		
Engine horsepower	26 c—v	25.6 hp
Piston displacement	1,279 cu cm	76.7 cu. ins.
Fuel tank capacity	25 liters	6.6 gal.
Highway fuel consumption		23.5 m.p.g.
Average terrain fuel consumption		

RADIO CAR
Fu. Kw. (Kfz. 2)

German nomenclature: Funkkraftwagen (Kfz. 2) mit
dem Einheitsfahrgestell I für leichter Pkw.

English designation: Radio car with standard chassis I
for light armored car.

Net weight	1,725 kg	3,802 lb.
Pay load	475 kg	1,047 lb.
Gross weight	2,200 kg	4,849 lb.
Weight: Front axle	1,050 kg	2,315 lb.
Weight: Rear axle	1,150 kg	2,535 lb.
Length (overall)	3,850 mm	12 ft., 7 ins.
Width (overall)	1,690 mm	5 ft., 6 ins.
Height (overall)	1,900 mm	6 ft., 3 ins.
Ground clearance	235 mm	9 1/4 ins.
Tread centers	1,400 mm	4 ft., 7 ins.
Wheelbase	2,400 mm	94 ins.
Wheel width	158 mm	6 1/4 ins.
Angle of approach		60°
Angle of departure		45°
Seating capacity		2
Fording depth	500 mm	19 7/8 ins.
Climbing ability		30°
Overturn gradient (lengthwise)		40°
Overturn gradient (crosswise)		30°
Turning radius	12/6.5 meters	39 ft., 4 ins. ft., 4 ins.
Trailer load		
Engine horsepower	45 c—v	44.4 hp
Piston displacement	2,000 cu cm	120 cu. ins.
Fuel tank capacity	60 liters	15.9 gal.
Highway fuel consumption		13.6 m.p.g.
Average terrain fuel consumption		9.4 m.p.g.

RADIO CAR
Fu. Kw. (Kfz. 2)

German nomenclature: Funkkraftwagen (Kfz. 2) mit Fahrgestell des mittleren Pkw. (o).

English designation: Radio car with special chassis for medium armored car (standard commercial vehicle).

Net weight	1,225 kg	2,700 lb.
Pay load	475 kg	1,047 lb.
Gross weight	1,700 kg	3,747 lb.
Weight: Front axle	820 kg	1,808 lb.
Weight: Rear axle	880 kg	1,940 lb.
Length (overall)	4,110 mm	13 ft., 6 ins.
Width (overall)	1,580 mm	5 ft., 2 ins.
Height (overall)	1,800 mm	5 ft., 11 ins.
Ground clearance	220 mm	8⅝ ins.
Tread centers	1,350 mm	4 ft., 5 ins.
Wheelbase	2,300 mm	90 ins.
Wheel width	160 mm	6¼ ins.
Angle of approach		50°
Angle of departure		30°
Seating capacity		2
Fording depth	400 mm	15¾ ins.
Climbing ability		17°
Overturn gradient (lengthwise)		45°
Overturn gradient (crosswise)		30°
Turning radius	12 meters	39 ft., 4 ins.
Trailer load		
Engine horsepower		
Piston displacement	2,000 cu cm	120 cu. ins.
Fuel tank capacity	60 liters	15.9 gal.
Highway fuel consumption		18.1 m.p.g.
Average terrain fuel consumption		9.8 m.p.g.

LIGHT SURVEY SECTION CAR
l. Messtr. Kw. (Kfz. 3)

German nomenclature: leichter Messtruppkraftwagen (Kfz. 3) mit Fahrgestell des leichter Pkw. (o).

English designation: Light survey section car with special chassis for light armored car (standard commercial vehicle).

Net weight	950 kg	2,094 lb.
Pay load	400 kg	882 lb.
Gross weight	1,350 kg	2,976 lb.
Weight: Front axle	600 kg	1,323 lb.
Weight: Rear axle	750 kg	1,653 lb.
Length (overall)	3,900 mm	12 ft., 9 ins.
Width (overall)	1,500 mm	4 ft., 11 ins.
Height (overall)	1,800 mm	5 ft., 11 ins.
Ground clearance	190 mm	7½ ins.
Tread centers	1,200 mm	47 ins.
Wheelbase	2,450 mm	96 ins.
Wheel width	125 mm	4⅞ ins.
Angle of approach		70°
Angle of departure		30°
Seating capacity		
Fording depth	500 mm	19⅞ ins.
Climbing ability		16°
Overturn gradient (lengthwise)		50°
Overturn gradient (crosswise)		40°
Turning radius	12 meters	39 ft., 4½ ins.
Trailer load		
Engine horsepower		
Piston displacement	1,500 cu cm	90 cu. ins.
Fuel tank capacity	40 liters	10.6 gal.
Highway fuel consumption		23.5 m.p.g.
Average terrain fuel consumption		15.7 m.p.g.

LIGHT SURVEY SECTION CAR
l. Messtr. Kw. (Kfz. 3)

German nomenclature: leichter Messtruppkraftwagen (Kfz. 3) mit Einheitsfahrgestell I für leichter Pkw.

English designation: Light survey section car with standard chassis I for light armored car.

Net weight	1,725 kg	3,802 lb.
Pay load	475 kg	1,047 lb.
Gross weight	2,200 kg	4,849 lb.
Weight: Front axle	1,050 kg	2,315 lb.
Weight: Rear axle	1,150 kg	2,535 lb.
Length (overall)	3,850 mm	12 ft., 7 ins.
Width (overall)	1,690 mm	5 ft., 6 ins.
Height (overall)	1,900 mm	6 ft., 3 ins.
Ground clearance	235 mm	9¼ ins.
Tread centers	1,400 mm	4 ft., 7 ins.
Wheelbase	2,400 mm	94 ins.
Wheel width	158 mm	6¼ ins.
Angle of approach		60°
Angle of departure		45°
Seating capacity		3
Fording depth	500 mm	19⅞ ins.
Climbing ability		30°
Overturn gradient (lengthwise)		40°
Overturn gradient (crosswise)		30°
Turning radius	12/6.5 meters	39 ft., 4 ins./ ft., 4 ins.
Trailer load		
Engine horsepower	45 c–v	44.4 hp
Piston displacement	3,000 cu cm	180 cu. ins.
Fuel tank capacity	60 liters	15.9 gal.
Highway fuel consumption		13.6 m.p.g.
Average terrain fuel consumption		9.4 m.p.g.

ANTIAIRCRAFT PROTECTION TRUCK
.Tr. Luftsch. Kw. (Kfz. 4)

German nomenclature: Truppenluftschutzkraftwagen (Kfz. 4) mit Einheitsfahrgestell I für leichter Pkw.

English designation: Antiaircraft protection truck with standard chassis I for light armored car.

Net weight	1,800 kg	3,968 lb.
Pay load	400 kg	882 lb.
Gross weight	2,200 kg	4,849 lb.
Weight: Front axle	1,000 kg	2,204 lb.
Weight: Rear axle	1,200 kg	2,645 lb.
Length (overall)	3,850 mm	12 ft., 7 ins.
Width (overall)	1,700 mm	5 ft., 7 ins.
Height (overall)	1,900 mm	6 ft., 3 ins.
Ground clearance	220 mm	8⅝ ins.
Tread centers	1,400 mm	4 ft., 7 ins.
Wheelbase	2,400 mm	94 ins.
Wheel width	158 mm	6¼ ins.
Angle of approach		60°
Angle of departure		45°
Seating capacity		2
Fording depth	500 mm	19⅞ ins.
Climbing ability		30°
Overturn gradient (lengthwise)		40°
Overturn gradient (crosswise)		30°
Turning radius	12/6.5 meters	39 ft., 4 ins. ft., 4 ins.
Trailer load		
Engine horsepower	45 c–v	44.4 hp
Piston displacement	2,000 cu cm	120 cu. ins.
Fuel tank capacity	60 liters	15.9 gal.
Highway fuel consumption		13.6 m.p.g.
Average terrain fuel consumption		9.4 m.p.g.

SMALL REPAIR VEHICLE
kl. Inst. Kw. (Kfz. 2/40)

Net weight	1,260 kg	2,777 lb.
Pay load	420 kg	926 lb.
Gross weight	1,680 kg	3,703 lb.
Weight: Front axle	750 kg	1,653 lb.
Weight: Rear axle	930 kg	2,050 lb.
Length (overall)	4,110 mm	13 ft., 6 ins.
Width (overall)	1,580 mm	5 ft., 2 ins.
Height (overall)	1,800 mm	5 ft., 11 ins.
Ground clearance	220 mm	8⅝ ins.
Tread centers	1,350 mm	4 ft., 5 ins.
Wheelbase	2,300 mm	90 ins.
Wheel width	160 mm	6¼ ins.
Angle of approach		50°
Angle of departure		30°
Seating capacity		2
Fording depth	400 mm	15¾ ins.
Climbing ability		17°
Overturn gradient (lengthwise)		45°
Overturn gradient (crosswise)		30°
Turning radius	12 meters	39 ft., 4 ins.
Trailer load		
Engine horsepower	45 c–v	44.4 hp
Piston displacement	2,000 cu cm	120 cu. ins.
Fuel tank capacity	60 liters	15.9 gal.
Highway fuel consumption		18.1 m.p.g.
Average terrain fuel consumption		9.8 m.p.g.

German nomenclature: kleiner Instandsetzungskraftwagen (Kfz. 2/40) mit Fahrgestell des mittleren Pkw. (o).

English designation: Small repair vehicle with special chassis for medium armored car (standard commercial vehicle).

SMALL REPAIR VEHICLE
kl. Inst. Kw. (Kfz. 2/40)

Net weight	1,750 kg	3,857 lb.
Pay load	450 kg	992 lb.
Gross weight	2,200 kg	4,849 lb.
Weight: Front axle	1,000 kg	2,204 lb.
Weight: Rear axle	1,200 kg	2,645 lb.
Length (overall)	3,850 mm	12 ft., 7 ins.
Width (overall)	1,690 mm	5 ft., 6 ins.
Height (overall)	1,900 mm	6 ft., 3 ins.
Ground clearance	235 mm	9¼ ins.
Tread centers	1,400 mm	4 ft., 7 ins.
Wheelbase	2,400 mm	94 ins.
Wheel width	160 mm	6¼ ins.
Angle of approach		60°
Angle of departure		45°
Seating capacity		2
Fording depth	500 mm	19⅞ ins.
Climbing ability		30°
Overturn gradient (lengthwise)		40°
Overturn gradient (crosswise)		30°
Turning radius	12/6.5 meters	39 ft., 4 ins./21 ft., 4 ins.
Trailer load		
Engine horsepower	45 c–v	44.4 hp
Piston displacement	3,000 cu cm	180 cu. ins.
Fuel tank capacity	60 liters	15.9 gal.
Highway fuel consumption		13.6 m.p.g.
Average terrain fuel consumption		9.4 m.p.g.

German nomenclature: kleiner Instandsetzungskraftwagen (Kfz. 2/40) mit Einheitsfahrgestell I für leichter Pkw.

English designation: Small repair vehicle with standard chassis I for light armored car.

DUMMY TANK
Pz. Kpfw. Nachb.

German nomenclature: Panzerkampfwagen-Nachbildung mit Fahrgestell des leichter Pkw. (o).

English designation: Dummy tank with special chassis I for light armored car (standard commercial vehicle).

Net weight	980 kg	2,160 lb.
Pay load	385 kg	848 lb.
Gross weight	1,365 kg	3,008 lb.
Weight: Front axle	565 kg	1,245 lb.
Weight: Rear axle	800 kg	1,764 lb.
Length (overall)	3,730 mm	12 ft., 3 ins.
Width (overall)	1,775 mm	5 ft., 10 ins.
Height (overall)	1,980 mm	6 ft., 6 ins.
Ground clearance	200 mm	7⅞ ins.
Tread centers	1,253 mm	4 ft., 1 in.
Wheelbase	2,460 mm	97 ins.
Wheel width	160 mm	6¼ ins.
Angle of approach		50°
Angle of departure		40°
Seating capacity		
Fording depth	400 mm	15¾ ins.
Climbing ability		28°
Overturn gradient (lengthwise)		
Overturn gradient (crosswise)		45°
Turning radius	1.3 meters	4 ft., 3 ins.
Trailer load		
Engine horsepower	28.5 c—v	28.1 hp
Piston displacement	1,279 cu cm	76.7 cu. ins.
Fuel tank capacity	25 liters	6.6 gal.
Highway fuel consumption		26.1 m.p.g.
Average terrain fuel consumption		18.1 m.p.g.

MEDIUM PERSONNEL CAR
m. Pkw. (o)

German nomenclature: mittlerer Personenkraftwagen (o).

English designation: Medium personnel car (standard commercial vehicle).

Net weight	1,950 kg	4,298 lb.
Pay load	600 kg	1,323 lb.
Gross weight	2,550 kg	5,622 lb.
Weight: Front axle	1,200 kg	2,645 lb.
Weight: Rear axle	1,350 kg	2,975 lb.
Length (overall)	5,000 mm	16 ft., 5 ins.
Width (overall)	1,800 mm	5 ft., 11 ins.
Height (overall)	1,700 mm	5 ft., 7 ins.
Ground clearance	150 mm	5⅞ ins.
Tread centers	1,420 mm	4 ft., 8 ins.
Wheelbase	3,350 mm	132 ins.
Wheel width	170 mm	6¾ ins.
Angle of approach		50°
Angle of departure		20°
Seating capacity		4
Fording depth	400 mm	15¾ ins.
Climbing ability		17°
Overturn gradient (lengthwise)		40°
Overturn gradient (crosswise)		30°
Turning radius	12 meters	39 ft., 4 ins.
Trailer load		
Engine horsepower	80 c—v	78.9 hp
Piston displacement	1,500—3,000 cu cm	90—180 cu. ir
Fuel tank capacity	80 liters	21.1 gal.
Highway fuel consumption		13.1/19.6 m.:
Average terrain fuel consumption		

MEDIUM CROSS-COUNTRY PERSONNEL CAR
m. gl. Pkw. (Kfz. 11)

German nomenclature: mittlerer geländegängiger Personenkraftwagen (Kfz. 11) mit Fahrgestell des mittleren Pkw.

English designation: Medium cross-country personnel car with special chassis for medium armored car.

Net weight	1,600 kg	3,527 lb.
Pay load	500 kg	1,102 lb.
Gross weight	2,100 kg	4,630 lb.
Weight: Front axle	900 kg	1,984 lb.
Weight: Rear axle	1,100 kg	2,425 lb.
Length (overall)	4,800 mm	15 ft., 9 ins.
Width (overall)	1,800 mm	5 ft., 11 ins.
Height (overall)		
Ground clearance	265 mm	10⅜ ins.
Tread centers	1,450 mm	4 ft., 9 ins.
Wheelbase	3,350 mm	132 ins.
Wheel width	170 mm	6¾ ins.
Angle of approach		60°
Angle of departure		45°
Seating capacity		3
Fording depth	600 mm	23⅝ ins.
Climbing ability		18°
Overturn gradient (lengthwise)		50°
Overturn gradient (crosswise)		35°
Turning radius	13 meters	42 ft., 8 ins.
Trailer load		
Engine horsepower	70 c–v	69 hp
Piston displacement	1,500–3,000 cu cm	90–180 cu. ins.
Fuel tank capacity	70 liters	18.5 gal.
Highway fuel consumption		11.7 m.p.g.
Average terrain fuel consumption		7.8 m.p.g.

MEDIUM CROSS-COUNTRY PERSONNEL CAR
m. gl. Pkw. m. Zgv. (Kfz. 12)

German nomenclature: mittlerer geländegängiger Personenkraftwagen mit Zugvorrichtung (Kfz. 12) mit Fahrgestell des mittleren Pkw. (o).

English designation: Medium cross-country personnel car with towing apparatus with special chassis for medium armored car (standard commercial vehicle).

Net weight	1,600 kg	3,527 lb.
Pay load	600 kg	1,323 lb.
Gross weight	2,200 kg	4,850 lb.
Weight: Front axle	900 kg	1,984 lb.
Weight: Rear axle	1,300 kg	2,865 lb.
Length (overall)	4,800 mm	15 ft., 7 ins.
Width (overall)	1,800 mm	5 ft., 11 ins.
Height (overall)	2,000 mm	6 ft., 7 ins.
Ground clearance	265 mm	10 ins.
Tread centers	450 mm	4 ft., 9 ins.
Wheelbase	3,350 mm	132 ins.
Wheel width	170 mm	6¾ ins.
Angle of approach		60°
Angle of departure		45°
Seating capacity		3
Fording depth	600 mm	23⅝ ins.
Climbing ability		18°
Overturn gradient (lengthwise)		50°
Overturn gradient (crosswise)		35°
Turning radius	12.5 meters	41 ft.
Trailer load	700 kg	1,543 lb.
Engine horsepower	70 c–v	69 hp
Piston displacement	1,500–3,400 cu cm	90–204 cu. ins.
Fuel tank capacity	70 liters	18.5 gal.
Highway fuel consumption		9.4 m.p.g.
Average terrain fuel consumption		6.7 m.p.g.

MEDIUM CROSS-COUNTRY CAR
m. gl. Pkw. (Kfz. 12)

Net weight	2,600 kg	5,732 lb.
Pay load	500 kg	1,102 lb.
Gross weight	3,100 kg	6,834 lb.
Weight: Front axle	1,300 kg	2,865 lb.
Weight: Rear axle	1,800 kg	3,968 lb.
Length (overall)	4,700 mm	15 ft., 5 ins.
Width (overall)	1,860 mm	6 ft., 1 in.
Height (overall)	2,070 mm	6 ft., 9 ins.
Ground clearance	250 mm	9⅞ ins.
Tread centers	1,520 mm	4 ft., 12 ins.
Wheelbase	3,100 mm	122 ins.
Wheel width	194 mm	7⅝ ins.
Angle of approach		60°
Angle of departure		40°
Seating capacity		3
Fording depth	550 mm	21⅝ ins.
Climbing ability		30°
Overturn gradient (lengthwise)		50°
Overturn gradient (crosswise)		30°
Turning radius	13 meters	42 ft., 8 ins.
Trailer load	700 kg	1,543 lb.
Engine horsepower	80 c–v	78.9 hp
Piston displacement	3,600 cu cm	216 cu. ins.
Fuel tank capacity	110 liters	29 gal.
Highway fuel consumption		9.4 m.p.g.
Average terrain fuel consumption		7.1 m.p.g.

German nomenclature: mittlerer geländegängiger Personenkraftwagen (Kfz. 12) mit Einheitsfahrgestell für mittleren Pkw.

English designation: Medium cross-country car with standard chassis for medium armored car.

SIGNAL COMMUNICATIONS CAR
Nachr. Kw. (Kfz. 15)

Net weight	2,000 kg	4,429 lb.
Pay load	600 kg	1,323 lb.
Gross weight	2,600 kg	5,732 lb.
Weight: Front axle	1,050 kg	2,315 lb.
Weight: Rear axle	1,550 kg	3,417 lb.
Length (overall)	4,800 mm	15 ft., 9 ins.
Width (overall)	1,800 mm	5 ft., 11 ins.
Height (overall)	1,850 mm	6 ft., ⅞ in.
Ground clearance	265 mm	10 ins.
Tread centers	1,450 mm	4 ft., 9 ins.
Wheelbase	3,350 mm	132 ins.
Wheel width	170 mm	6¾ ins.
Angle of approach		60°
Angle of departure		45°
Seating capacity		3
Fording depth	550 mm	21⅝ ins.
Climbing ability		18°
Overturn gradient (lengthwise)		50°
Overturn gradient (crosswise)		30°
Turning radius	13 meters	42 ft., 8 ins.
Trailer load	700 kg	1,543 lb.
Engine horsepower	70 c–v	69 hp
Piston displacement	3,500 cu cm	210 cu. ins.
Fuel tank capacity	80 liters	21.1 gal.
Highway fuel consumption		10.7 m.p.g.
Average terrain fuel consumption		7.8 m.p.g.

German nomenclature: Nachrichtenkraftwagen (Kfz. 15) mit Fahrgestell des mittleren Pkw. (o).

English designation: Signal communications car with special chassis for medium armored car (standard commercial vehicle).

SIGNAL COMMUNICATIONS CAR
Nachr. Kw. (Kfz. 15)

German nomenclature: Nachrichtenkraftwagen (Kfz. 15) mit Einheitsfahrgestell für mittleren Panzerkraftwagen (o).

English designation: Signal communications car with standard chassis for medium armored car (standard commercial vehicle).

Net weight	2,600 kg	5,732 lb.
Pay load	700 kg	1,543 lb.
Gross weight	3,300 kg	7,275 lb.
Weight: Front axle	1,400 kg	3,086 lb.
Weight: Rear axle	1,900 kg	4,188 lb.
Length (overall)	4,700 mm	15 ft., 5 ins.
Width (overall)	1,860 mm	6 ft., 1 in.
Height (overall)	2,070 mm	6 ft., 9 ins.
Ground clearance	250 mm	9⅞ ins.
Tread centers	1,520 mm	5 ft.
Wheelbase	3,100 mm	122 ins.
Wheel width	194 mm	7⅝ ins.
Angle of approach		60°
Angle of departure		40°
Seating capacity		3
Fording depth	550 mm	21⅝ ins.
Climbing ability		30°
Overturn gradient (lengthwise)		50°
Overturn gradient (crosswise)		30°
Turning radius	13 meters	42 ft., 8 ins.
Trailer load	700 kg	1,543 lb.
Engine horsepower	80 c–v	78.9 hp
Piston displacement	3,600 cu cm	216 cu. ins.
Fuel tank capacity	110 liters	29 gal.
Highway fuel consumption		9.1 m.p.g.
Average terrain fuel consumption		7.1 m.p.g.

RADIO CAR
Fu. Kw. (Kfz. 15)

German nomenclature: Funkkraftwagen (Kfz. 15) mit Einheitsfahrgestell für mittleren Pkw.

English designation: Radio car with standard chassis for medium armored car.

Net weight	2,500 kg	5,512 lb.
Pay load	800 kg	1,764 lb.
Gross weight	3,300 kg	7,275 lb.
Weight: Front axle	1,400 kg	3,086 lb.
Weight: Rear axle	1,900 kg	4,188 lb.
Length (overall)	4,700 mm	15 ft., 5 ins.
Width (overall)	1,860 mm	6 ft., 1 in.
Height (overall)	2,070 mm	6 ft., 9 ins.
Ground clearance	250 mm	9⅞ ins.
Tread centers	1,520 mm	5 ft.
Wheelbase	3,100 mm	122 ins.
Wheel width	194 mm	7⅝ ins.
Angle of approach		60°
Angle of departure		40°
Seating capacity		
Fording depth	550 mm	21⅝ ins.
Climbing ability		30°
Overturn gradient (lengthwise)		50°
Overturn gradient (crosswise)		30°
Turning radius	13 meters	42 ft., 8 ins.
Trailer load	700 kg	1,549 lb.
Engine horsepower	80 c–v	78.9 hp
Piston displacement	3,600 cu cm	216 cu. ins.
Fuel tank capacity	110 liters	29 gal.
Highway fuel consumption		9.4 m.p.g.
Average terrain fuel consumption		7.1 m.p.g.

MEDIUM FLASH AND SOUND RANGING CAR
m. Messtr. Kw. (Kfz. 16)

German nomenclature: mittlerer Messtruppkraftwagen (Kfz. 16) mit Fahrgestell des mittleren Pkw (o).

English designation: Medium flash and sound ranging car with special chassis for medium armored car (standard commercial vehicle).

Net weight	1,760 kg	3,879 lb.
Pay load	590 kg	1,301 lb.
Gross weight	2,350 kg	5,181 lb.
Weight: Front axle	980 kg	2,160 lb.
Weight: Rear axle	1,370 kg	3,020 lb.
Length (overall)	4,850 mm	15 ft., 11 ins.
Width (overall)	1,830 mm	6 ft.
Height (overall)	1,960 mm	6 ft., 5 ins.
Ground clearance	265 mm	10 ins.
Tread centers	1,450 mm	4 ft., 9 ins.
Wheelbase	3,000 mm	118 ins.
Wheel width	170 mm	6¾ ins.
Angle of approach		60°
Angle of departure		45°
Seating capacity		3
Fording depth	550 mm	21⅝ ins.
Climbing ability		15°
Overturn gradient (lengthwise)		50°
Overturn gradient (crosswise)		20°
Turning radius	14 meters	46 ft., 4 ins.
Trailer load	700 kg	1,549 lb.
Engine horsepower	70 c–v	69 hp
Piston displacement	3,000 cu cm	180 cu. ins.
Fuel tank capacity	54 liters	14.3 gal.
Highway fuel consumption		10.4 m.p.g.
Average terrain fuel consumption		7.8 m.p.g.

MEDIUM FLASH AND SOUND RANGING CAR
m. Messtr. Kw. (Kfz. 16)

German nomenclature: mittlerer Messtruppkraftwagen (Kfz. 16) mit Einheitsfahrgestell für mittleren Pkw. (o). Vorwarnerkraftwagen (Kfz. 16/1) mit Einheitsfahrgestell für mittleren Pkw.

English designation: Medium flash and sound ranging car with special chassis for medium armored car (standard commercial vehicle).
Advance scout car with standard chassis for medium armored car.

Net weight	2,500 kg	5,512 lb.
Pay load	800 kg	1,764 lb.
Gross weight	3,300 kg	7,275 lb.
Weight: Front axle	1,400 kg	3,086 lb.
Weight: Rear axle	1,900 kg	4,188 lb.
Length (overall)	4,700 mm	15 ft., 5 ins.
Width (overall)	1,860 mm	6 ft., 1 in.
Height (overall)	2,050 mm	6 ft., 9 ins.
Ground clearance	250 mm	9⅞ ins.
Tread centers	1,520 mm	5 ft.
Wheelbase	3,100 mm	122 ins.
Wheel width	194 mm	7⅝ ins.
Angle of approach		60°
Angle of departure		40°
Seating capacity		3
Fording depth	550 mm	21⅝ ins.
Climbing ability		30°
Overturn gradient (lengthwise)		50°
Overturn gradient (crosswise)		30°
Turning radius	12.50 meters	41 ft.
Trailer load	700 kg	1,549 lb.
Engine horsepower	80 c–v	78.9 hp
Piston displacement	3,600 cu cm	216 cu. ins.
Fuel tank capacity	110 liters	29 gal.
Highway fuel consumption		9.1 m.p.g.
Average terrain fuel consumption		7.1 m.p.g.

TELEPHONE EXCHANGE CAR
Fsp. Betr. Kw. (Kfz. 17)

German nomenclature: Fernsprech-Betriebskraftwagen (Kfz. 17) mit Einheitsfahrgestell für mittleren Pkw.

English designation: Telephone exchange car with standard chassis for medium armored car.

Net weight	2,600 kg	5,732 lb.
Pay load	1,080 kg	2,381 lb.
Gross weight	3,680 kg	8,113 lb.
Weight: Front axle	1,630 kg	3,593 lb.
Weight: Rear axle	2,050 kg	4,519 lb.
Length (overall)	4,800 mm	15 ft., 9 ins.
Width (overall)	1,800 mm	5 ft., 11 ins.
Height (overall)	1,850 mm	7 ft.
Ground clearance	250 mm	9⅞ ins.
Tread centers	1,520 mm	5 ft.
Wheelbase	3,100 mm	122 ins.
Wheel width	194 mm	7⅝ ins.
Angle of approach		60°
Angle of departure		40°
Seating capacity		3
Fording depth	550 mm	21⅝ ins.
Climbing ability		30°
Overturn gradient (lengthwise)		50°
Overturn gradient (crosswise)		30°
Turning radius	12.5 meters	41 ft.
Trailer load	700 kg	1,549 lb.
Engine horsepower	60 c–v	59.2 hp
Piston displacement	3,000 cu cm	180 cu. ins.
Fuel tank capacity	110 liters	29 gal.
Highway fuel consumption		9.1 m.p.g.
Average terrain fuel consumption.		7.1 m.p.g.

RADIO CAR
Fu. Kw. (Kfz. 17)

German nomenclature: Funkkraftwagen (Kfz. 17) mit dem Fahrgestell des mittleren Pkw. (o).

English designation: Radio car with special chassis for medium armored car (standard commercial vehicle).

Net weight	2,050 kg	4,519 lb.
Pay load	800 kg	1,764 lb.
Gross weight	2,850 kg	6,283 lb.
Weight: Front axle	1,050 kg	2,315 lb.
Weight: Rear axle	1,800 kg	3,968 lb.
Length (overall)	4,750 mm	15 ft., 7 ins.
Width (overall)	1,800 mm	5 ft., 11 ins.
Height (overall)	1,950 mm	6 ft., 5 ins.
Ground clearance	265 mm	10 ins.
Tread centers	1,450 mm	4 ft., 9 ins.
Wheelbase	3,200 mm	126 ins.
Wheel width	170 mm	6¾ ins.
Angle of approach		60°
Angle of departure		45°
Seating capacity		3
Fording depth	550 mm	21⅝ ins.
Climbing ability		15°
Overturn gradient (lengthwise)		50°
Overturn gradient (crosswise)		30°
Turning radius	14 meters	46 ft., 4 ins.
Trailer load	700 kg	1,549 lb.
Engine horsepower	70 c–v	69 hp
Piston displacement	3,400 cu cm	204 cu. in.
Fuel tank capacity	110 liters	29 gal.
Highway fuel consumption		9.4 m.p.g.
Average terrain fuel consumption..		7.1 m.p.g.

RADIO CAR
Fu. Kw. (Kfz. 17)

German nomenclature: Funkkraftwagen (Kfz. 17) mit Einheitsfahrgestell für mittleren Pkw.

English designation: Radio car with standard chassis for medium armored car.

Net weight	2,650 kg	5,842 lb.
Pay load	1,000 kg	2,204 lb.
Gross weight	3,650 kg	8,047 lb.
Weight: Front axle	1,600 kg	3,527 lb.
Weight: Rear axle	2,050 kg	4,519 lb.
Length (overall)	4,800 mm	15 ft., 9 ins.
Width (overall)	1,860 mm	6 ft., 1 in.
Height (overall)	2,250 mm	7 ft., 4 ins.
Ground clearance	250 mm	9⅞ ins.
Tread centers	1,520 mm	5 ft.
Wheelbase	3,100 mm	122 ins.
Wheel width	194 mm	7⅝ ins.
Angle of approach		60°
Angle of departure		40°
Seating capacity		3
Fording depth	550 mm	21⅝ ins.
Climbing ability		30°
Overturn gradient (lengthwise)		50°
Overturn gradient (crosswise)		30°
Turning radius	12.5 meters	41 ft.
Trailer load	700 kg	1,549 lb.
Engine horsepower	80 c–v	78.9 hp
Piston displacement	3,600 cu cm	216 cu. ins.
Fuel tank capacity	110 liters	29 gal.
Highway fuel consumption		9.4 m.p.g.
Average terrain fuel consumption		7.1 m.p.g.

RADIO CAR
Fu. Kw. (Kfz. 17/1)

German nomenclature: Funkkraftwagen (Kfz. 17/1) mit Einheitsfahrgestell für mittleren Pkw.

English designation: Radio car with standard chassis for medium armored car.

Net weight	2,670 kg	5,886 lb.
Pay load	930 kg	2,050 lb.
Gross weight	3,600 kg	7,937 lb.
Weight: Front axle	1,600 kg	3,527 lb.
Weight: Rear axle	2,000 kg	4,409 lb.
Length (overall)	4,700 mm	15 ft., 5 ins.
Width (overall)	1,840 mm	6 ft.
Height (overall)	2,070 mm	6 ft., 9 ins.
Ground clearance	250 mm	9⅞ ins.
Tread centers	1,520 mm	5 ft.
Wheelbase	3,100 mm	122 ins.
Wheel width	194 mm	7⅝ ins.
Angle of approach		60°
Angle of departure		40°
Seating capacity		3
Fording depth	550 mm	21⅝ ins.
Climbing ability		30°
Overturn gradient (lengthwise)		50°
Overturn gradient (crosswise)		30°
Turning radius	12.5 meters	41 ft.
Trailer load	700 kg	1,549 lb.
Engine horsepower	80 c–v	78.9 hp
Piston displacement	3,600 cu cm	216 cu. ins.
Fuel tank capacity	110 liters	29 gal.
Highway fuel consumption		9.4 m.p.g.
Average terrain fuel consumption		7.1 m.p.g.

CABLE SURVEYING CAR
Kabelmess. Kw. (Kfz. 17)

German nomenclature: Kabelmesskraftwagen (Kfz. 17) mit Einheitsfahrgestell für mittleren Pkw.

English designation: Cable surveying car with standard chassis for medium armored car.

Net weight	2,600 kg	5,732 lb.
Pay load	925 kg	2,039 lb.
Gross weight	3,525 kg	7,771 lb.
Weight: Front axle	1,740 kg	3,836 lb.
Weight: Rear axle	1,785 kg	3,934 lb.
Length (overall)	4,800 mm	15 ft., 9 ins.
Width (overall)	1,800 mm	5 ft., 11 ins.
Height (overall)	1,850 mm	6 ft., 1 in.
Ground clearance	250 mm	9⅞ ins.
Tread centers	1,520 mm	5 ft.
Wheelbase	3,100 mm	122 ins.
Wheel width	194 mm	7⅝ ins.
Angle of approach		60°
Angle of departure		40°
Seating capacity		3
Fording depth	550 mm	21⅝ ins.
Climbing ability		30°
Overturn gradient (lengthwise)		50°
Overturn gradient (crosswise)		30°
Turning radius	12.5 meters	41 ft.
Trailer load	700 kg	1,549 lb.
Engine horsepower	80 c–v	78.9 hp
Piston displacement	3,600 cu cm	216 cu ins.
Fuel tank capacity	110 liters	29 gal.
Highway fuel consumption		9.4 m.p.g.
Average terrain fuel consumption		7.1 m.p.g.

EMERGENCY REPAIR CAR
Gef. Kw. (Kfz. 18)

German nomenclature: Gefechtskraftwagen (Kfz. 18) mit Fahrgestell des mittleren Pkw. (o).

English designation: Emergency repair car with special chassis for medium armored car (standard commercial vehicle).

Net weight	1,610 kg	3,549 lb.
Pay load	1,070 kg	2,358 lb.
Gross weight	2,680 kg	5,908 lb.
Weight: Front axle	1,240 kg	2,733 lb.
Weight: Rear axle	1,440 kg	3,174 lb.
Length (overall)	4,400 mm	14 ft., 5 ins.
Width (overall)	1,700 mm	5 ft., 7 ins.
Height (overall)	1,820 mm	6 ft.
Ground clearance	265 mm	10⅞ ins.
Tread centers	1,450 mm	4 ft., 9 ins.
Wheelbase	2,900 mm	114 ins.
Wheel width	170 mm	6¾ ins.
Angle of approach		60°
Angle of departure		45°
Seating capacity		1
Fording depth	550 mm	21⅝ ins.
Climbing ability		18°
Overturn gradient (lengthwise)		50°
Overturn gradient (crosswise)		20°
Turning radius	14 meters	46 ft., 4 ins.
Trailer load	700 kg	1,549 lb.
Engine horsepower	60 c–v	59.2 hp
Piston displacement	3,000 cu cm	180 cu. ins.
Fuel tank capacity	70 liters	18.5 gal.
Highway fuel consumption		11.7 m.p.g.
Average terrain fuel consumption		7.8 m.p.g.

HEAVY PERSONNEL CAR
s. Pkw. (o)

German nomenclature: schwerer Personenkraftwagen (o).

English designation: Heavy personnel car (standard commercial vehicle).

Net weight	2,500 kg	5,512 lb.
Pay load	600 kg	1,322 lb.
Gross weight	3,100 kg	6,834 lb.
Weight: Front axle	1,350 kg	2,975 lb.
Weight: Rear axle	1,750 kg	3,857 lb.
Length (overall)	5,600 mm	18 ft., 4 ins.
Width (overall)	1,850 mm	6 ft., ⅞ in.
Height (overall)	1,800 mm	5 ft., 11 ins.
Ground clearance	100 mm	3⅞ ins.
Tread centers	1,520 mm	5 ft.
Wheelbase	3,750 mm	148 ins.
Wheel width	195 mm	7⅝ ins.
Angle of approach		60°
Angle of departure		50°
Seating capacity		6
Fording depth	400 mm	15¾ ins.
Climbing ability		17°
Overturn gradient (lengthwise)		50°
Overturn gradient (crosswise)		35°
Turning radius	15 meters	49 ft., 2 ins.
Trailer load		
Engine horsepower	70 c—v	69 hp
Piston displacement	3,000 cu cm	180 cu. ins.
Fuel tank capacity	100 liters	26.4 gal.
Highway fuel consumption		7.8 m.p.g.
Average terrain fuel consumption		

HEAVY CROSS-COUNTRY PERSONNEL CAR
s. gl. Pkw. (Kfz. 21)

German nomenclature: schwerer geländegängiger Personenkraftwagen (Kfz. 21) mit Fahrgestell des schweres geländegängiger Pkw. (o).

English designation: Heavy cross-country personnel car with special chassis for heavy cross-country armored car (standard commercial vehicle).

Net weight	2,550 kg	5,622 lb.
Pay load	600 kg	1,323 lb.
Gross weight	3,150 kg	6,945 lb.
Weight: Front axle	1,350 kg	2,975 lb.
Weight: Rear axle	1,800 kg	3,968 lb.
Length (overall)	5,600 mm	18 ft., 4 ins.
Width (overall)	2,350 mm	7 ft., 8 ins.
Height (overall)	2,150 mm	7 ft.
Ground clearance	130 mm	5⅛ ins.
Tread centers	1,450 mm	4 ft., 9 ins.
	1,930 mm	6 ft., 4 ins.
Wheelbase	3,470 mm	137 ins.
Wheel width	170/350 mm	6¾/13¾ ins.
Angle of approach		60°
Angle of departure		45°
Seating capacity		7
Fording depth	800 mm	31½ ins.
Climbing ability		25°
Overturn gradient (lengthwise)		50°
Overturn gradient (crosswise)		35°
Turning radius	17 meters	55 ft., 2 ins.
Trailer load		
Engine horsepower	90 c—v	88.8 hp
Piston displacement	3,000 cu cm	180 cu. ins.
Fuel tank capacity	100 liters	26.4 gal.
Highway fuel consumption		7.8 m.p.g.
Average terrain fuel consumption		6.2 m.p.g.

HEAVY CROSS-COUNTRY PERSONNEL CAR
gl. Pkw. (Kfz. 21)

Net weight	2,630 kg	5,798 lb.
Pay load	670 kg	1,477 lb.
Gross weight	3,300 kg	7,275 lb.
Weight: Front axle	1,440 kg	3,175 lb.
Weight: Rear axle	1,900 kg	4,188 lb.
Length (overall)	4,850 mm	15 ft., 11 ins.
Width (overall)	1,860 mm	6 ft., 2 ins.
Height (overall)	2,050 mm	6 ft., 9 ins.
Ground clearance	230 mm	9 ins.
Tread centers	1,520 mm	5 ft.
Wheelbase	3,100 mm	122 ins.
Wheel width	194 mm	7⅝ ins.
Angle of approach		60°
Angle of departure		40°
Seating capacity		5
Fording depth	550 mm	21⅝ ins.
Climbing ability		30°
Overturn gradient (lengthwise)		50°
Overturn gradient (crosswise)		30°
Turning radius	12.5 meters	41 ft.
Trailer load	700 kg	1,543 lb.
Engine horsepower	80 c—v	78.9 hp
Piston displacement	3,600 cu cm	216 cu. ins.
Fuel tank capacity	110 liters	29 gal.
Highway fuel consumption		8.4 m.p.g.
Average terrain fuel consumption..		6.7 m.p.g.

German nomenclature: schwerer geländegängiger Personenkraftwagen (6-sitzig) (Kfz. 21) mit Einheitsfahrgestell für mittleren Pkw.

English designation: Heavy cross-country personnel car (6-passenger) with standard chassis for medium armored car.

TELEPHONE TRUCK
sp. Kw. (Kfz. 23)

Net weight	3,000 kg	6,614 lb.
Pay load	1,500 kg	3,307 lb.
Gross weight	4,500 kg	9,921 lb.
Weight: Front axle	2,230 kg	4,916 lb.
Weight: Rear axle	2,270 kg	5,004 lb.
Length (overall)	4,850 mm	15 ft., 11 ins.
Width (overall)	2,000 mm	6 ft., 7 ins.
Height (overall)	2,040 mm	6 ft., 9 ins.
Ground clearance	230 mm	9 ins.
Tread centers	1,640 mm	5 ft., 4 ins.
Wheelbase	3,000 mm	118 ins.
Wheel width	215 mm	8½ ins.
Angle of approach		55°
Angle of departure		45°
Seating capacity		6
Fording depth	500 mm	19⅞ ins.
Climbing ability		25°
Overturn gradient (lengthwise)		45°
Overturn gradient (crosswise)		30°
Turning radius	13.5 meters	44 ft., 3 ins.
Trailer load		
Engine horsepower	90 c—v	88.8 hp
Piston displacement	4,000 cu cm	240 cu. ins.
Fuel tank capacity	120 liters	31.7 gal.
Highway fuel consumption		6.7 m.p.g.
Average terrain fuel consumption..		5.2 m.p.g.

German nomenclature: Fernsprechkraftwagen (Kfz. 23) mit Einheitsfahrgestell II für schwerer Pkw.

English designation: Telephone truck with standard chassis II for heavy armored car.

MAINTENANCE TRUCK
Verst. Kw. (Kfz. 24)

German nomenclature: Verstarkerkraftwagen (Kfz. 24) mit Einheitsfahrgestell II für schwerer Pkw.

English designation: Maintenance truck with standard chassis II for heavy armored car.

Net weight	3,150 kg	6,945 lb.
Pay load	1,750 kg	3,857 lb.
Gross weight	4,300 kg	9,480 lb.
Weight: Front axle	2,000 kg	4,409 lb.
Weight: Rear axle	2,330 kg	5,137 lb.
Length (overall)	4,850 mm	15 ft., 11 ins.
Width (overall)	2,000 mm	6 ft., 7 ins.
Height (overall)	2,760 mm	9 ft., 5/8 in.
Ground clearance	230 mm	9 ins.
Tread centers	1,640 mm	5 ft., 4 ins.
Wheelbase	3,000 mm	118 ins.
Wheel width	210 mm	8¼ ins.
Angle of approach		55°
Angle of departure		45°
Seating capacity		
Fording depth	500 mm	19⅞ ins.
Climbing ability		25°
Overturn gradient (lengthwise)		45°
Overturn gradient (crosswise)		30°
Turning radius	16.5 meters	54 ft., 1 in.
Engine horsepower	90 c–v	88.8 hp
Piston displacement	4,000 cu cm	240 cu. ins.
Fuel tank capacity	120 liters	31.7 gal.
Highway fuel consumption		6.7 m.p.g.
Average terrain fuel consumption		5.2 m.p.g.

LIGHT SEARCHLIGHT TRUCK I
l. Scheinw. Kw. I (Kfz. 83)

German nomenclature: leichter Scheinwerferkraftwagen I (Kfz. 83) mit Fahrgestell des leichter geländegängiger Pkw. (o).

English designation: Light searchlight truck I with special chassis for light cross-country armored car (standard commercial vehicle).

Net weight	2,600 kg	5,732 lb.
Pay load	1,180 kg	2,601 lb.
Gross weight	3,780 kg	8,333 lb.
Weight: Front axle	1,060 kg	2,336 lb.
Weight: Rear axle	1,360 kg	2,998 lb.
Length (overall)	4,950 mm	16 ft., 3 ins.
Width (overall)	1,950 mm	6 ft., 5 ins.
Height (overall)	2,300 mm	7 ft., 6 ins.
Ground clearance	200 mm	7⅞ ins.
Tread centers	1,580 mm	5 ft., 2 ins.
	1,565 mm	5 ft., 1 in.
	1,565 mm	5 ft., 1 in.
Wheelbase	2,445/900 mm	96/35 ins.
Wheel width	190 mm	7½ ins.
Angle of approach		60°
Angle of departure		40°
Seating capacity		5
Fording depth	600 mm	23⅝ ins.
Climbing ability		20°
Overturn gradient (lengthwise)		50°
Overturn gradient (crosswise)		30°
Turning radius	16 meters	52 ft., 6 ins.
Trailer load		
Engine horsepower	65 c–v	64.1 hp
Piston displacement	3,500 cu cm	210 cu. ins.
Fuel tank capacity	110 liters	29 gal.
Highway fuel consumption		7.8 m.p.g.
Average terrain fuel consumption		4.7 m.p.g.

LIGHT SEARCHLIGHT TRUCK I
Scheinw. Kw. I (Kfz. 83)

German nomenclature: leichter Scheinwerferkraftwagen I (Kfz. 83) mit Einheitsfahrgestell II für schwerer Pkw.

English designation: Light searchlight truck I with standard chassis II for heavy armored car.

Net weight	3,150 kg	6,945 lb.
Pay load	1,180 kg	2,601 lb.
Gross weight	4,330 kg	9,546 lb.
Weight: Front axle	2,100 kg	4,630 lb.
Weight: Rear axle	2,230 kg	4,916 lb.
Length (overall)	4,850 mm	15 ft., 11 ins.
Width (overall)	2,000 mm	6 ft., 7 ins.
Height (overall)	2,040 mm	6 ft., 8 ins.
Ground clearance	230 mm	9 ins.
Tread centers	1,640 mm	5 ft., 4 ins.
Wheelbase	3,000 mm	118 ins.
Wheel width	215 mm	8½ ins.
Angle of approach		55°
Angle of departure		45°
Seating capacity		5
Fording depth	500 mm	19⅞ ins.
Climbing ability		25°
Overturn gradient (lengthwise)		45°
Overturn gradient (crosswise)		30°
Turning radius	16.5 meters	54 ft., 1 in.
Trailer load	1,000 kg	2,205 lb.
Engine horsepower	90 c–v	88.8 hp
Piston displacement	4,000 cu cm	240 cu. ins.
Fuel tank capacity	120 liters	31.7 gal.
Highway fuel consumption		5.2 m.p.g.
Average terrain fuel consumption		6.7 m.p.g.

LIGHT SEARCHLIGHT TRUCK II
Scheinw. Kw. II (Kfz. 83)

German nomenclature: leichter Scheinwerferkraftwagen II (Kfz. 83) mit Fahrgestell des leichter geländegängiger Pkw. (o).

English designation: Light searchlight truck II with special chassis for light cross-country armored car (standard commercial vehicle).

Net weight	2,600 kg	5,732 lb.
Pay load	1,180 kg	2,601 lb.
Gross weight	3,780 kg	8,333 lb.
Weight: Front axle	1,060 kg	2,336 lb.
Weight: Rear axle	1,360 kg	2,998 lb.
Length (overall)	4,950 mm	16 ft., 3 ins.
Width (overall)	1,950 mm	6 ft., 5 ins.
Height (overall)	2,300 mm	7 ft., 6 ins.
Ground clearance	200 mm	7⅞ ins.
Tread centers	1,580 mm	5 ft., 2 ins.
	1,565 mm	5 ft., 1 in.
	1,565 mm	5 ft., 1 in.
Wheelbase	2,445/900 mm	96/35 ins.
Wheel width	190 mm	7½ ins.
Angle of approach		60°
Angle of departure		40°
Seating capacity		5
Fording depth	600 mm	23⅝ ins.
Climbing ability		20°
Overturn gradient (lengthwise)		50°
Overturn gradient (crosswise)		30°
Turning radius	16 meters	52 ft., 6 ins.
Trailer load		
Engine horsepower	65 c–v	64.1 hp
Piston displacement	3,500 cu cm	210 cu. ins.
Fuel tank capacity	110 liters	29 gal.
Highway fuel consumption		7.8 m.p.g.
Average terrain fuel consumption		4.7 m.p.g.

LIGHT SEARCHLIGHT TRUCK II

l. Scheinw. Kw. II (Kfz. 83)

German nomenclature: leichter Scheinwerferkraftwagen II (Kfz. 83) mit Einheitsfahrgestell II für schwerer Pkw.

English designation: Light searchlight truck II with standard chassis II for heavy armored car.

Net weight	3,150 kg	6,945 lb.
Pay load	1,180 kg	2,601 lb.
Gross weight	4,330 kg	9,546 lb.
Weight: Front axle	2,100 kg	4,630 lb.
Weight: Rear axle	2,230 kg	4,916 lb.
Length (overall)	4,850 mm	15 ft., 11 ins.
Width (overall)	2,000 mm	6 ft., 7 ins.
Height (overall)	2,040 mm	6 ft., 8 ins.
Ground clearance	230 mm	9 ins.
Tread centers	1,640 mm	5 ft., 4 ins.
Wheelbase	3,000 mm	118 ins.
Wheel width	215 mm	8½ ins.
Angle of approach		55°
Angle of departure		45°
Seating capacity		5
Fording depth	500 mm	19⅞ ins.
Climbing ability		25°
Overturn gradient (lengthwise)		45°
Overturn gradient (crosswise)		30°
Turning radius	16.5 meters	54 ft., 1 in.
Trailer load	1,000 kg	2,205 lb.
Engine horsepower	90 c—v	88.8 hp
Piston displacement	4,000 cu cm	240 cu. ins.
Fuel tank capacity	120 liters	31.7 gal.
Highway fuel consumption		6.7 m.p.g.
Average terrain fuel consumption		5.2 m.p.g.

AMBULANCE

Kr. Kw. (Kfz. 31)

German nomenclature: Krankenkraftwagen (Kfz. 31) mit Fahrgestell des leichter Lastkraftwagen (o).

English designation: Ambulance with special chassis for light truck (standard commercial vehicle).

Net weight	2,400 kg	5,292 lb.
Pay load	1,000 kg	2,204 lb.
Gross weight	3,400 kg	7,496 lb.
Weight: Front axle	1,100 kg	2,425 lb.
Weight: Rear axle	2,300 kg	5,071 lb.
Length (overall)	5,400 mm	17 ft., 8 ins.
Width (overall)	2,050 mm	6 ft., 9 ins.
Height (overall)	2,300 mm	7 ft., 6 ins.
Ground clearance	230 mm	9 ins.
Tread centers	1,600 mm	5 ft., 3 ins.
Wheelbase	3,600 mm	142 ins.
Wheel width	170 mm	6¾ ins.
Angle of approach		60°
Angle of departure		50°
Seating capacity		8
Fording depth	500 mm	19⅞ ins.
Climbing ability		12°
Overturn gradient (lengthwise)		50°
Overturn gradient (crosswise)		30°
Turning radius	16 meters	52 ft., 6 ins.
Trailer load		
Engine horsepower	40 c—v	39.5 hp
Piston displacement	3,000 cu cm	180 cu. ins.
Fuel tank capacity	110 liters	29 gal.
Highway fuel consumption		6.7 m.p.g.
Average terrain fuel consumption		5.2 m.p.g.

AMBULANCE
Kr. Kw. (Kfz. 31)

Net weight	3,050 kg	6,724 lb.
Pay loan	1,200 kg	2,645 lb.
Gross weight	4,250 kg	9,368 lb.
Weight: Front axle	2,000 kg	4,409 lb.
Weight: Rear axle	2,250 kg	4,960 lb.
Length (overall)	4,850 mm	15 ft., 11 ins.
Width (overall)	2,000 mm	6 ft. 7 ins.
Height (overall)	2,100 mm	6 ft., 10 ins.
Ground clearance	230 mm	9 ins.
Tread centers	1,640 mm	5 ft., 4 ins.
Wheelbase	3,000 mm	118 ins.
Wheel width	215 mm	8½ ins.
Angle of approach		55°
Angle of departure		45°
Seating capacity		9
Fording depth	500 mm	19⅞ ins.
Climbing ability		25°
Overturn gradient (lengthwise)		45°
Overturn gradient (crosswise)		50°
Turning radius	13.5 meters	44 ft., 3 ins.
Trailer load	1,000 kg	2,205 lb.
Engine horsepower	90 c–v	88.8 hp
Pisotn displacement	4,000 cu cm	240 cu. ins.
Fuel tank capacity	120 liters	31.7 gal.
Highway fuel consumption		6.7 m.p.g.
Average terrain fuel consumption..	6,724 lb.	5.2 m.p.g.

German nomenclature: Krankenkraftwagen (Kfz. 31) mit Einheitsfahrgestell II für schwerer Pkw.

English designation: Ambulance with standard chassis II for heavy armored car.

MAINTENANCE TRUCK
Protzkw. (Kfz. 69)

Net weight	2,700 kg	5,952 lb.
Pay load	1,00 kg	2,204 lb.
Gross weight	3,700 kg	8,157 lb.
Weight Front axle	1,070 kg	2,358 lb.
Weight: Rear axle	1,315 kg	2,899 lb.
Length (overall)	5,000 mm	16 ft., 5 ins.
Width (overall)	1,900 mm	6 ft., 3 ins.
Height (overall)	1,800 mm	5 ft., 11 ins.
Ground clearance	220 mm	8⅝ ins.
Tread centers	1,580 mm	5 ft., 2 ins.
	1,665 mm	5 ft., 1 in.
	1,565 mm	5 ft., 1 in.
Wheelbase	2,445/900 mm	96 96 3/5 ins.
Wheel width	190 mm	7½ ins.
Angle of approach		50°
Angle of departure		40°
Seating capacity		
Fording depth	600 mm	23⅝ ins.
Climbing ability		20°
Overturn gradient (lengthwise)		50°
Overturn gradient (crosswise)		30°
Turning radius	16 meters	52 ft., 6 ins.
Trailer load	1,000 kg	2,205 lb.
Engine horsepower	65 c–v	64.1 hp
Pitson displacement	3,500 cu cm	210 cu. ins.
Fuel tank capacity	110 liters	29 gal.
Highway fuel consumption		7.8 m.p.g.
Average terrain fuel consumption		4.7 m.p.g.

German nomenclature: Protzkraftwagen (Kfz. 69) mit Fahrgestell des leichter geländegängiger Lastkraftwagen (o).

English designation: Maintenance truck with special chassis for light cross-country truck (standard commercial vehicle).

LIMBER TRUCK
Protzkw. (Kfz. 69)

German nomenclautre: Protzkraftwagen (Kfz. 69) mit Einheitsfahrgestell II für schwerer Pkw.

English designation: Limber truck with standard chassis II for heavy armored car.

Net weight	3,150 kg	6,944 lb.
Pay load	1,050 kg	2,314 lb.
Gross weight	4,200 kg	9,258 lb.
Weight: Front axle	2,000 kg	4,409 lb.
Weight: Rear axle	2,200 kg	4,850 lb.
Length (overall)	4,850 mm	15 ft., 11 ins.
Width (overall)	2,000 mm	6 ft., 7 ins.
Height (overall)	2,040 mm	6 ft., 8 ins.
Ground clearance	230 mm	9 ins.
Tread centers	1,640 mm	5 ft., 4 ins.
Wheelbase	3,000 mm	118 ins.
Wheel width	215 mm	8½ ins.
Angle of approach		55°
Angle of departure		45°
Seating capacity		5
Fording depth	500 mm	19⅞ ins.
Climbing ability		25°
Overturn gradient (lengthwise)		45°
Overturn gradient (crosswise)		45°
Turning radius	16.5 meters	54 ft., ⅛ in.
Trailer load	1,000 kg	2,205 lb.
Engine horsepower	90 c–v	88.8 hp
Piston displacement	4,000 cu cm	240 cu. ins.
Fuel tank capacity	120 liters	31.7 gal.
Highway fuel consmption		6.7 m.p.g.
Average terrain fuel consumption		5.2 m.p.g.

PERSONNEL CARRIER
Mannsch. Kw. (Kfz. 70)

German nomenclature: Mannschaftskraftwagen (Kfz. 70) mit Fahrgestell des leichter geländegängiger Lastkraftwagen (o).

English designation: Personnel carrier with special chassis for light cross-country truck (standard commercial vehicle).

Net weight	2,600 kg	5,732 lb.
Pay load	1,150 kg	2,535 lb.
Gross weight	3,750 kg	8,267 lb.
Weight: Front axle	1,070 kg	2,358 lb.
Weight: Rear axle	2,790 kg	6,150 lb.
Length (overall)	4,950 mm	16 ft., 3 ins.
Width (overall)	1,950 mm	6 ft., 5 ins.
Height (overall)	2,300 mm	7 ft., 6 ins.
Ground clearance	220 mm	8⅝ ins.
Tread centers	1,580 mm	5 ft., 2 ins.
	1,565 mm	5 ft., 1 in.
	1,565 mm	5 ft., 1 in.
Wheelbase	2,445/900 mm	96–35 in.
Wheel width	190 mm	7½ ins.
Angle of approach		50°
Angle of departure		40°
Seating capacity		
Fording depth	600 mm	23⅝ ins.
Climbing ability		20°
Overturn gradient (lengthwise)		50°
Overturn gradient (crosswise)		30°
Turning radius	16 meters	52 ft., 6 ins
Trailer load	1,00 kg	2,205 lb.
Engine horsepower	65 c–v	64.1 hp
Piston displacement	3,500 cu cm	210 cu. ins.
Fuel tank capacity	110 liters	29 gal.
Highway fuel consumption		7.8 m.p.g.
Average terrain fuel consumption		4.7 m.p.g.

RECONNAISSANCE CAR
Mannsch. Kw. (Kfz. 70)

German nomenclature: Mannschaftskraftwagen (Kfz. 70) mit Einheitsfahrgestell II für schwerer Pkw.

English designation: Reconnaissance car with standard chassis II for heavy armored car.

Net weight	3,150 kg	6,944 lb.
Pay load	1,050 kg	2,314 lb.
Gross weight	4,200 kg	9,258 lb.
Weight: Front axle	2,000 kg	4,409 lb.
Weight: Rear axle	2,200 kg	4,850 lb.
Length (overall)	4,850 mm	15 ft., 11 ins.
Width (overall)	2,000 mm	6 ft., 7 ins.
Height (overall)	2,040 mm	6 ft., 8 ins.
Ground clearance	230 mm	9 ins.
Tread centers	1,640 mm	5 ft., 4 ins.
Wheelbase	3,000 mm	118 ins.
Wheel width	215 mm	8½ ins.
Angle of approach		55°
Angle of departure		45°
Seating capacity		7
Fording depth	500 mm	19⅞ ins.
Climbing ability		25°
Overturn gradient (lengthwise)		45°
Overturn gradient (crosswise)		30°
Turning radius	13.5 meters	44 ft., 3 ins.
Trailer load	1,000 kg	2,205 lb.
Engine horsepower	90 c–v	88.8 hp
Piston displacement	4,000 cu cm	240 cu. ins.
Fuel tank capacity	120 liters	31.7 gal.
Highway fuel consumption		6.7 m.p.g.
Average terrain fuel consumption		5.2 m.p.g.

ANTIAIRCRAFT UNIT LIGHT TRUCK
Flkw. (Kfz. 81)

German nomenclature: leichter Flakkraftwagen (Kfz. 81) mit Fahrgestell des leichter geländegängiger Lastkraftwagen (o).

English designation: Antiaircraft unit light truck with special chassis for light cross-country truck (standard commercial vehicle).

Net weight	2,600 kg	5,732 lb.
Pay load	1,150 kg	2,535 lb.
Gross weight	3,750 kg	8,267 lb.
Weight: Front axle	1,060 kg	2,336 lb.
Weight: Right axle	1,45 kg	2,950 lb.
Length (overall)	4,950 mm	16 ft., 3 ins.
Width (overall)	1,950 mm	6 ft., 5 ins.
Height(overall)	2,300 mm	7 ft., 6 ins.
Central	200 mm	7⅞ ins.
Ground clearance	225 mm	8⅞ ins.
Tread centers	1,580 mm	5 ft., 2 ins.
	1,565 mm	5 ft., 1 in.
	1.565 mm	5 ft., 1 in.
Wheelbase	2,470–860 mm	97 ins./34 ins.
Wheel width	190 mm	7½ ins.
Angle of approach		60°
Angle of departure		40°
Seating capacity		7
Fording depth	600 mm	23⅝ ins.
Climbing ability		20°
Overturn gradient (lengthwise)		50°
Overturn gradient (crosswise)		30°
Turning radius	16 meters	52 ft., 6 ins.
Trailer load	800 kg	1,764 lb.
Engine horsepower	65 c–v	64.1 hp
Piston displacement	3,500 cu cm	210 cu. ins.
Fuel tank capacity	110 liters	90 gal
Highway fuel consumption		7.8 m.p.g.
Average terrain fuel consumption		4.7 m.p.g.

ANTIAIRCRAFT UNIT LIGHT CAR
l. Flkw. (Kfz. 81)

German nomenclature: leichter Flakkraftwagen (Kfz. 81) mit Einheitsfahrgestell II für schwerer Pkw.

English designation: Antiaircraft unit light car with standard chassis II for heavy armored car.

Net weight	3,150 kg	6,945 lb.
Pay load	1,250 kg	2,755 lb.
Gross weight	4,400 kg	9,700 lb.
Weight: Front axle	2,100 kg	4,630 lb.
Weight: Rear axle	2,300 kg	5,0717 lb.
Length (overall)	4,850 mm	15 ft., 11 ins.
Width (overall)	2,000 mm	6 ft., 7 ins.
Height (overall)	2,040 mm	6 ft., 8 ins.
Ground clearance	230 mm	9 ins.
Tread centers	1,640 mm	5 ft., 4 ins.
Wheelbase	3,000 mm	118 ins.
Wheel width	215 mm	8½ ins.
Angle of approach		55°
Angle of departure		45°
Seating capacity		8
Fording depth	500 mm	19⅞ ins.
Climbing ability		25°
Overturn gradient (lengthwise)		45°
Overturn gradient (crosswise)		30°
Turning radius	13.5 meters	44 ft., 3 ins.
Trailer load	1,000 kg	2,205 lb.
Engine horsepower	90 c–v	88.8 hp
Pieston displacement	4,000 cu cm	240 cu. ins.
Fuel tank capacity	120 liters	31.7 gal.
Highway fuel consumption		6.7 m.p.g.
Average terrain fuel consumption		5.2 m.p.g.

LIGHT COMMERCIAL TRUCK (OPEN)
l. Klw. off. (o)

German nomenclature: leichter Lastkraftwagen offen (o).

English designation: Light commercial truck, open (standard commercial vehicle).

Net weight	3,000 kg	6,614 lb.
Pay load	2,000 kg	4,409 lb.
Gross weight	5,000 kg	11,023 lb.
Weight: Front axle	1,800 kg	3,968 lb.
Weight: Rear axle	3,200 kg	7,055 lb.
Length (overall)	6,600 mm	21 ft., 7 ins.
Width (overall)	2,200 mm	7 ft., 3 ins.
Height (overall)	2,600 mm	8 ft., 6 ins.
Ground clearance	200 mm	7⅞ ins.
Tread centers	1,600 mm	5 ft., 3 ins.
	2,000 mm	6 ft., 7 ins.
Wheelbase	3,600 mm	142 ins.
Wheel width	170 mm	6¾ ins.
Angle of approach		50°
Angle of departure		50°
Seating capacity		20
Fording depth	500 mm	19⅞ ins.
Climbing ability		15°
Overturn gradient (lengthwise)		50°
Overturn gradient (crosswise)		30°
Turning radius	16 meters	52 ft., 6 ins
Trailer load	1,000 kg	2,205 lb.
Engine horsepower	65 c–v	64.1 hp
Piston displacement	3,500 cu cm	210 cu. ins.
Fuel tank capacity	120 liters	31.7 gal.
Highway fuel consumption		6.7/9.4 m.p

LIGHT TRUCK
Lkw. mit geschl. Aufbau (o)

Net weight	2,500 kg	5,512 lb.
Pay load	2,000 kg	4,409 lb.
Gross weight	4,500 kg	9,921 lb.
Weight: Front axle	1,500 kg	3,307 lb.
Weight: Rear axle	3,000 kg	6,614 lb.
Length (overall)	6,000 mm	19 ft., 8 ins.
Width (overall)	2,200 mm	7 ft., 3 ins.
Height (overall)	2,600 mm	8 ft., 6 ins.
Ground clearance	200 mm	7⅞ ins.
Tread centers	1,600 mm	5 ft., 3 ins.
	1,800 mm	5 ft., 11 ins.
Wheelbase	3,600 mm	142 ins.
Wheel width	170 mm	6¾ ins.
Angle of approach		60°
Angle of departure		40°
Seating capacity		19
Fording depth	500 mm	19⅞ ins.
Climbing ability		15°
Overturn gradient (lengthwise)		50°
Overturn gradient (crosswise)		30°
Turning radius		
Trailer load	1,000 kg	2,205 lb.
Engine horsepower	65 c–v	64.1 hp
Piston displacement	3,500 cu cm	210 cu. ins.
Fuel tank capacity	120 liters	31.7 gal.
Highway fuel consumption		5.9 m.p.g.
Average terrain fuel consumption..		7.8 m.p.g.

German nomenclature: leichter Lastkraftwagen mit geschlossenem Aufbau (o).

English designation: Light truck with locked super-structure (standard commercial chassis).

LIGHT CROSS-COUNTRY TRUCK (OPEN)
gl. Lkw. off. (o) — Pi. Kw. III

Net weight	3,300 kg	7,275 lb.
Pay load	1,500 kg	3,307 lb.
Gross weight	4,800 kg	10,582 lb.
Weight: Front axle	1,100 kg	2,425 lb.
Weight: Rear axle	1,850 kg	4,078 lb.
Length (overall)	6,000 mm	19 ft., 8 ins.
Width (overall)	2,100 mm	6 ft., 11 ins.
Height (overall)	2,400 mm	7 ft., 10 ins.
Ground clearance	200 mm	7⅞ ins.
Tread centers	1,600 mm	5 ft., 3 ins.
	1,800 mm	5 ft., 11 ins.
Wheelbase	3,000/950 mm	118/37 ins.
Wheel width	170 mm	6¾ ins.
Angle of approach		60°
Angle of departure		40°
Seating capacity		12
Fording depth	600 mm	23⅝ ins.
Climbing ability		20°
Overturn gradient (lengthwise)		50°
Overturn gradient (crosswise)		30°
Turning radius	19.5 meters	63 ft., 11¾ ins.
Trailer load	1,800 kg	3,968 lb.
Engine horsepower	65 c–v	64.1 hp
Piston displacement	3,500 cu cm	204 cu. ins.
Fuel tank capacity	110 liters	29 gal.
Highway fuel consumption		6.7 m.p.g.
Average terrain fuel consumption		4.7 m.p.g.

German nomenclature: leichter geländegängiger Lastkraftwagen, offen (o).
Pionierkraftwagen III (leichter geländegängiger Lkw. (o)).

English designation: Light cross-country truck, open. Engineers' truck III (light cross-country truck), (standard commercial chassis).

LIGHT CROSS-COUNTRY TRUCK (OPEN)

l. gl. Lkw. off. — Kw. III

Net weight	5,000 kg	11,023 lb.
Pay load	2,500 kg	5,512 lb.
Gross weight	7,500 kg	16,534 lb.
Weight: Front axle	2,300 kg	5,071 lb.
Weight: Rear axle	2,600 kg	5,732 lb.
Length (overall)	5,850 mm	19 ft., 2 ins.
Width (overall)	2,200 mm	7 ft., 2 ins.
Height (overall)	2,400 mm	7 ft., 10 ins.
Ground clearance	250 mm	9⅞ ins.
Tread centers	1,720 mm	5 ft., 8 ins.
Wheelbase	3,100/1,100 mm	122/43 ins.
Wheel width	215 mm	8½ ins.
Angle of approach		60°
Angle of departure		40°
Seating capacity		25
Fording depth	800 mm	31½ ins.
Climbing ability		30°
Overturn gradient (lengthwise)		50°
Overturn gradient (crosswise)		30°
Turning radius	17 meters	55 ft., 2 ins.
Trailer load	3,500 kg	7,716 lb.
Engine horsepower	85 c-v	83.8 hp
Piston displacement	6,234 cu cm	374 cu. ins.
Fuel tank capacity	120 liters	31.7 gal.
Highway fuel consumption		7.3 m.p.g.
Average terrain fuel consumption		5.2 m.p.g.

German nomenclature: leichter geländegängiger Lastkraftwagen, offen.

Pionierkraftwagen III mit Einheitsfahrgestell für leichter Lastkraftwagen.

English designation: Light cross-country truck, open.

Engineers' truck III with standard chassis for light truck.

FIELD TELEPHONE CABLE TRUCK

Ff. Kabel-Kw.

Net weight	5,000 kg	11,023 lb.
Pay load	2,140 kg	4,718 lb.
Gross weight	7,140 kg	15,741 lb.
Weight: Front axle	2,160 kg	4,762 lb.
Weight: Rear axle	2,490 kg	5,490 lb.
Length (overall)	5,850 mm	19 ft., 2 ins.
Width (overall)	2,200 mm	7 ft., 2 ins.
Height (overall)	2,400 mm	7 ft., 10 ins.
Ground clearance	280 mm	11 ins.
Tread centers	1,720 mm	5 ft., 8 ins.
Wheelbase	3,100/1,100 mm	122 ins./43 i.
Wheel width	215 mm	8½ ins.
Tire size		
Angle of approach		60°
Angle of departure		40°
Seating capacity		25
Fording depth	800 mm	31½ ins.
Climbing ability		30°
Overturn gradient (lengthwise)		50°
Overturn gradient (crosswise)		30°
Turning radius	17 meters	55 ft., 2¼ in.
Trailer load	3,500 kg	7,716 lb.
Lifting power of winch		
Engine horsepower		
Piston displacement	6,234 cu cm	374 cu. ins.
Fuel tank capacity	120 liters	31.7 gal.
Highway fuel consumption		7.3 m.p.g.
Average terrain fuel consumption		5.2 m.p.g.

German nomenclature: Feldfernkabelkraftwagen mit Einheitsfahrgestell für leichter Lastkraftwagen.

English designation: Field telephone cable truck with standard chassis for light truck.

RECONNAISSANCE TRUCK
Beob. Kw. (Kfz. 76)

German nomenclature: Beobachtungskraftwagen (Kfz. 76) mit Fahrgestell des leichter geländegängiger Lastkraftwagen (o).

English designation: Reconnaissance truck with special chassis for light cross-country truck.

Net weight	3,925 kg	8,652 lb.
Pay load	795 kg	1,753 lb.
Gross weight	4,720 kg	10,405 lb.
Weight: Front axle	1,430 kg	3,152 lb.
Weight: Rear axle	1,645 kg	3,626 lb.
Length (overall)	5,390 mm	17 ft., 8 ins.
Width (overall)	2,220 mm	7 ft., 3 ins.
Height (overall)	2,350 mm	7 ft., 8 ins.
Ground clearance	225 mm	8⅞ ins.
Tread centers	1,600 mm	5 ft., 3 ins.
	1,800 mm	5 ft., 11 ins.
	1,800 mm	5 ft., 11 ins.
Wheelbase	3,000/950 mm	118/37 ins.
Wheel width	170–350 mm	6¾–13¾ ins.
Angle of approach		60°
Angle of departure		40°
Seating capacity		9
Fording depth	600 mm	23⅝ ins.
Climbing ability		20°
Overturn gradient (lengthwise)		50°
Overturn gradient (crosswise)		30°
Turning radius	19.5 meters	63 ft., 12 ins.
Trailer load		
Engine horsepower	65 c–v	64.1 hp
Piston displacement	3,500 cu cm	210 cu. ins.
Fuel tank capacity	110 liters	29 gal.
Highway fuel consumption		5.9 m.p.g.
Average terrain fuel consumption		4.7 m.p.g.

TELEPHONE TRUCK
Fsp. Kw. (Kfz. 77)

German nomenclature: Fernsprechkraftwagen (Kfz. 77) mit Fahrgestell des leichter geländegängiger Lastkraftwagen (o).

English designation: Telephone truck with special chassis for light truck.

Net weight	3,330 kg	7,341 lb.
Pay load	1,585 kg	3,494 lb.
Gross weight	4,915 kg	10,835 lb.
Weight: Front axle	1,715 kg	3,780 lb.
Weight: Rear axle	1,600 kg	3,527 lb.
Length (overall)	5,750 mm	18 ft., 10 ins.
Width (overall)	2,220 mm	7 ft., 3 ins.
Height (overall)	2,350 mm	7 ft., 8 ins.
Ground clearance	225 mm	8⅞ ins.
Tread centers	1,600 mm	5 ft., 3 ins.
	1,800 mm	5 ft., 11 ins.
	1,800 mm	5 ft., 11 ins.
Wheelbase	3,000/950 mm	118/37 ins.
Wheel width	170–350 mm	6¾–13¾ ins.
Angle of approach		60°
Angle of departure		40°
Seating capacity		6
Fording depth	600 mm	23⅝ ins.
Climbing ability		20°
Overturn gradient (lengthwise)		50°
Overturn gradient (crosswise)		30°
Turning radius	19.5 meters	63 ft., 12 ins.
Engine horsepower	65 c–v	64.1 hp
Piston displacement	3,500 cu cm	210 cu. ins.
Fuel tank capacity	110 liters	29 gal.
Highway fuel consumption		5.9 m.p.g.
Average terrain fuel consumption		4.3 m.p.g.

TELEPHONE GENERATOR TRUCK
Fsp. Betr. Kw. (Kfz. 61)

German nomenclature: Fernsprechbetriebskraftwagen (Kfz. 61) mit Einheitsfahrgestell für leichter Lastkraftwagen.

English designation: Telephone generator truck with standard chassis for light truck.

Net weight	5,000 kg	11,023 lb.
Pay load	2,420 kg	5,334 lb.
Gross weight	7,420 kg	16,358 lb.
Weight: Front axle	2,750 kg	6,062 lb.
Weight: Rear axle	2,335 kg	5,148 lb.
Length (overall)	5,850 mm	19 ft., 2 ins.
Width (overall)	2,200 mm	7 ft., 2 ins.
Height (overall)	2,760 mm	9 ft.
Ground clearance	280 mm	11 ins.
Tread centers	1,600 mm	5 ft., 3 ins.
	1,800 mm	5 ft., 11 ins.
Wheelbase	3,100/1,100 mm	122/43 ins.
Wheel width	215–350 mm	8½–13¾ ins.
Angle of approach		60°
Angle of departure		40°
Seating capacity		4
Fording depth	800 mm	31½ ins.
Climbing ability		30°
Overturn gradient (lengthwise)		50°
Overturn gradient (crosswise)		30°
Turning radius	17 meters	55 ft., 2 ins.
Trailer load	3,500 kg	7,716 lb.
Engine horsepower	85 c–v	83.8 hp
Piston displacement	6,234 cu cm	374 cu. ins.
Fuel tank capacity	120 liters	31.7 gal.
Highway fuel consumption		7.3 m.p.g.
Average terrain fuel consumption		5.2 m.p.g.

TELETYPE TRUCK
Fernschr. Kw. (Kfz. 61)

German nomenclature: Fernschreibkraftwagen (Kfz. 61) mit Fahrgestell des leichter geländegängiger Lastkraftwagen (o).

English designation: Teletype truck with special chassis for light cross-country truck.

Net weight	3,880 kg	8,553 lb.
Pay load	1,100 kg	2,425 lb.
Gross weight	4,980 kg	10,978 lb.
Weigh:t Front axle	1,280 kg	2,821 lb.
Weight: Rear axle, each	1,850 kg	4,078 lb.
Length (overall)	5,700 mm	18 ft., 8 ins.
Width (overall)	2,050 mm	6 ft., 8 ins.
Height (overall)	2,760 mm	9 ft.
Ground clearance	225 mm	8⅞ ins.
Tread centers	1,600 mm	5 ft., 3 ins.
	1,800 mm	5 ft., 11 ins.
	1,800 mm	5 ft., 11 ins.
Wheelbase	3,000/950 mm	118/37 ins.
Wheel width	350/170 mm	13¾/6¾ ins.
Angle of approach		60°
Angle of departure		40°
Seating capacity		3
Fording depth	600 mm	23⅝ ins.
Climbing ability		20°
Overturn gradient (lengthwise)		60°
Overturn gradient (crosswise)		30°
Turning radius	19.5 meters	64 ft.
Trailer load		
Engine horsepower	65 c–v	64.1 hp
Piston displacement	3,500 cu cm	210 cu. ins.
Fuel tank capacity	110 liters	29 gal.
Highway fuel consumption		5.9 m.p.g.
Average terrain fuel consumption		4.3 m.p.g.

RADIO TRUCK
Fu. Kw. (Kfz. 61)

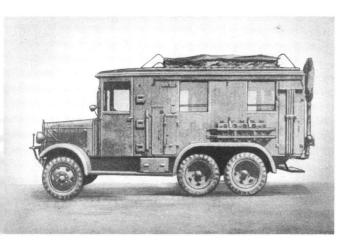

Net weight	3,700 kg	8,157 lb.
Pay load	1,300 kg	2,866 lb.
Gross weight	5,000 kg	11,020 lb.
Weight: Front axle	1,400 kg	3,086 lb.
Weight: Rear axle, each	1,800 kg	3,968 lb.
Length (overall)	5,630 mm	18 ft., 5 ins.
Width (overall)	2,060 mm	6 ft., 9 ins.
Height (overall)	2,650 mm	8 ft., 8 ins.
Ground clearance	225 mm	8⅞ ins.
Tread centers	1,600 mm	5 ft., 3 ins.
	1,800 mm	5 ft., 11 ins.
	1,800 mm	5 ft., 11 ins.
Wheelbase	3,000/950 mm	118/37 ins.
Wheel width	170/350 mm	6⅝/13¾ ins.
Angle of approach		60°
Angle of departure		40°
Seating capacity		
Fording depth	600 mm	23⅝ ins.
Climbing ability		20°
Overturn gradient (lengthwise)		50°
Overturn gradient (crosswise)		40°
Turning radius	19.5 meters	64 ft.
Trailer load		
Engine horsepower	65 c–v	64.1 hp
Piston displacement	3,500 cu cm	7,716 cu. ins.
Fuel tank capacity	110 liters	29 gal.
Highway fuel consumption		5.9 m.p.g.
Average terrain fuel consumption		4.3 m.p.g.

German nomenclature: Funkkraftwagen (Kfz. 61) mit Fehrgestell des leichter geländegängiger Lastkraftwagen (o).

English designation: Radio truck with special chassis for light cross-country truck.

RADIO TRUCK
Fu. Kw. (Kzw./Lgw.) (Kfz. 302)

Net weight	6,040 kg	13,315 lb.
Pay load	1,260 kg	2,777 lb.
Gross weight	7,300 kg	16,093 lb.
Weight: Front axle	2,200 kg	4,850 lb.
Weight: Rear axle, each	2,550 kg	5,622 lb.
Length (overall)	6,000 mm	19 ft., 8 ins.
Width (overall)	2,200 mm	7 ft., 2 ins.
Height (overall)	2,950 mm	9 ft., 8 ins.
Ground clearance	280 mm	11¼ ins.
Tread centers	1,720 mm	5 ft., 8 ins.
Wheelbase	3,100/1,100 mm	122/43 ins.
Wheel width	215 mm	8½ ins.
Angle of approach		60°
Angle of departure		42°
Seating capacity		
Fording depth	800 mm	31½ ins.
Climbing ability		30°
Overturn gradient (lengthwise)		50°
Overturn gradient (crosswise)		30°
Turning radius	17 meters	55 ft., 2 ins.
Trailer load	3,500 kg	7,716 lb.
Engine horsepower	85 c–v	83.8 hp
Piston displacement	6,234 cu cm	374 cu. ins.
Fuel tank capacity	120 liters	31.7 gal.
Highway fuel consumption		7.3 m.p.g.
Average terrain fuel consumption		5.2 m.p.g.

German nomenclature: Funkkraftwagen (Kurzwellan/ Langwellan) (Kfz. 302) mit Einheitsfahrgestell für leichter Lastkraftwagen.

English designation: Radio truck with standard chassis for light truck.

RADIO ANTENNA TRUCK
Fu. Mastkw. (Kfz. 68)

Net weight	3,750 kg	8,267 lb.
Pay load	800 kg	1.764 lb.
Gross weight	4,550 kg	10,031 lb.
Weight: Front axle	1,100 kg	2,425 lb.
Weight: Rear axle, each	1,725 kg	3,802 lb.
Length (overall)	5,680 mm	18 ft., 7 ins.
Width (overall)	2,080 mm	6 ft., 10 ins.
Height (overall)	2,600 mm	8 ft., 6 ins.
Ground clearance	200 mm	7⅞ ins.
Tread centers	1,600 mm	5 ft., 3 ins.
	1,800 mm	5 ft., 11 ins.
	1,800 mm	5 ft., 11 ins.
Wheelbase	3,000/950 mm	118/37 ins.
Wheel width	170/350 mm	6¾/13¾ ins.
Angle of approach		60°
Angle of departure		40°
Seating capacity		
Fording depth	600 mm	23⅝ ins.
Climbing ability		20°
Overturn gradient (lengthwise)		50°
Overturn gradient (crosswise)		30°
Turning radius	19.5 meters	64 ft.
Trailer load		
Engine horsepower	65 c–v	64.1 hp
Piston displacement	3,500 cu cm	210 cu. ins.
Fuel tank capacity	110 liters	29 gal.
Highway fuel consumption		5.9 m.p.g.
Average terrain fuel consumption		4.3 m.p.g.

German nomenclature: Funkmastkraftwagen (Kfz. 68) mit Fahrgestell des leichter geländegängiger Lastkraftwagen (o).

English designation: Radio antenna truck with special chassis for light cross-country truck.

RADIO ANTENNA TRUCK
Fu. Mastkw. (Kfz. 68)

Net weight	5,430 kg	11,968 lb.
Pay load	1,520 kg	3,351 lb.
Gross weight	7,050 kg	15,542 lb.
Weight: Front axle	2,250 kg	4,960 lb.
Weight: Rear axle, each	1,950 kg	4,298 lb.
Length (overall)	5,900 mm	19 ft., 4 ins.
Width (overall)	2,210 mm	7 ft., 3 ins.
Height (overall)	2,800 mm	9 ft., 2 ins.
Ground clearance	280 mm	11¼ ins.
Tread centers	1,680 mm	5 ft., 6 ins.
Wheelbase	3,070/1,150 mm	121/45 ins.
Wheel width	215 mm	8½ ins.
Angle of approach		60°
Angle of departure		40°
Seating capacity		9
Fording depth	800 mm	31½ ins.
Climbing ability		30°
Overturn gradient (lengthwise)		50°
Overturn gradient (crosswise)		30°
Turning radius	17 meters	55 ft., 2 ins.
Trailer load	3,500 kg	7,716 lb.
Engine horsepower	85 c–v	83.8 hp
Piston displacement	6,234 cu cm	374 cu. ins.
Fuel tank capacity	120 liters	31.7 gal.
Highway fuel consumption		7.3 m.p.g.
Average terrain fuel consumption		5.2 m.p.g.

German nomenclature: Funkmastkraftwagen (Kfz. 68) mit Einheitsfahrgestell für leichter Lastkraftwagen.

English designation: Radio antenna truck with standard chassis for light truck.

RADIO BEACON TRUCK

Peilkw. a (Kfz. 61)

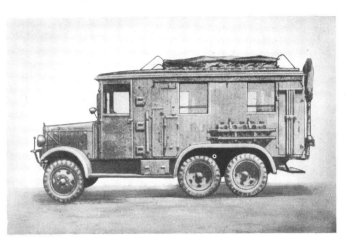

German nomenclature: Peilkraftwagen a (Kfz. 61) mit Fahrgestell des leichter geländegängiger Lastkraftwagen (o).

English designation: Radio beacon truck with special chassis for light cross-country truck.

Net weight	3,950 kg	8,707 lb.
Pay load	1,280 kg	2,822 lb.
Gross weight	5,230 kg	11,529 lb.
Weight: Front axle	1,230 kg	2,711 lb.
Weight: Rear axle, each	2,000 kg	4,409 lb.
Length (overall)	5,600 mm	18 ft., 4 ins.
Width (overall)	2,020 mm	6 ft., 7 ins.
Height (overall)	2,750 mm	9 ft.
Ground clearance	225 mm	8⅞ ins.
Tread centers	1,620 mm	5 ft., 3 ins.
	1,800 mm	5 ft., 11 ins.
	1,800 mm	5 ft., 11 ins.
Wheelbase	3,000/950 mm	118/37 ins.
Wheel width	170/350 mm	6¾/13¾ ins.
Angle of approach		60°
Angle of departure		40°
Seating capacity		
Fording depth	600 mm	23⅝ ins.
Climbing ability		14–16°
Overturn gradient (lengthwise)		60°
Overturn gradient (crosswise)		30°
Turning radius	19.5 meters	64 ft.
Trailer load		
Engine horsepower	65 c–v	64.1 hp
Piston displacement	3,950 cu cm	237 cu. ins.
Fuel tank capacity	110 liters	29 gal.
Highway fuel consumption		5.9 m.p.g.
Average terrain fuel consumption		4.3 m.p.g.

CABLE SURVEYING TRUCK

Kabelmess-Kw. (Kfz. 61)

German nomenclature: Kabelmesskraftwagen (Kfz. 61) mit Einheitsfahrgestell für leichter Lastkraftwagen.

English designation: Cable surveying truck with standard chassis for light truck.

Net weight		
Pay load		
Gross weight		
Weight: Front axle		
Weight: Rear axle, each		
Length (overall)	5,850 mm	19 ft., 2 ins.
Width (overall)	2,200 mm	7 ft., 2 ins.
Height (overall)	2,760 mm	9 ft.
Ground clearance	280 mm	11¼ ins.
Tread centers	1,720 mm	5 ft., 8 ins.
Wheelbase	3,100/1,100 mm	122/43 ins.
Wheel width	215 mm	8½ ins.
Angle of approach		60°
Angle of departure		40°
Seating capacity		4
Fording depth	800 mm	31½ ins.
Climbing ability		30°
Overturn gradient (lengthwise)		50°
Overturn gradient (crosswise)		30°
Turning radius	17 meters	55 ft., 2 ins.
Trailer load	3,500 kg	7,716 lb.
Engine horsepower	85 c–v	83.8 hp
Piston displacement	6,234 cu cm	374 cu. ins.
Fuel tank capacity	120 liters	31.7 gal.
Highway fuel consumption		7.3 m.p.g.
Average terrain fuel consumption		5.2 m.p.g.

MAINTENANCE TRUCK

Verst. Kw. (Kfz. 61)

Net weight	3,570 kg	7,870 lb.
Pay load	1,900 kg	4,188 lb.
Gross weight	5,470 kg	12,057 lb.
Weight: Front axle	1,590 kg	3,505 lb.
Weight: Rear axle, each	1,940 kg	4,276 lb.
Length (overall)	5,700 mm	18 ft., 8 ins.
Width (overall)	2,100 mm	6 ft., 10 ins.
Height (overall)	2,760 mm	9 ft.
Ground clearance	225 mm	8⅞ ins.
Tread centers	1,600 mm	5 ft., 3 ins.
	1,800 mm	5 ft., 11 ins.
	1,800 mm	5 ft., 11 ins.
Wheelbase	3,000/950 mm	118/37 ins.
Wheel width	170/350 mm	6¾/13¾ ins.
Angle of approach		60°
Angle of departure		40°
Seating capacity		3
Fording depth	600 mm	23⅝ ins.
Climbing ability		20°
Overturn gradient (lengthwise)		60°
Overturn gradient (crosswise)		30°
Turning radius	13.5 meters	44 ft., 3 ins.
Trailer load		
Engine horsepower	65 c—v	64.1 hp
Piston displacement	3,500 cu cm	210 cu. ins.
Fuel tank capacity	110 liters	29 gal.
Highway fuel consumption		5.9 m.p.g.
Average terrain fuel consumption		4.3 m.p.g.

German nomenclature: Verstärkerkraftwagen (Kfz. 61) mit Fahrgestell des leichter geländegängiger Lastkraftwagen (o).

English designation: Maintenance truck with special chassis for light cross-country truck.

MAINTENANCE TRUCK

Verst. Kw. (Kfz. 61)

Net weight	5,200 kg	11,463 lb.
Pay load	1,630 kg	3,593 lb.
Gross weight	6,830 kg	15,056 lb.
Weight: Front axle	2,490 kg	5,490 lb.
Weight: Rear axle, each	2,170 kg	4,784 lb.
Length (overall)	5,850 mm	19 ft., 2 ins.
Width (overall)	2,200 mm	7 ft., 7 ins.
Height (overall)	2,760 mm	9 ft.
Ground clearance	280 mm	11¼ ins.
Tread centers	1,720 mm	5 ft., 7 ins.
Wheelbase	3,100/1,100 mm	122/43 ins.
Wheel width	215 mm	8½ ins.
Angle of approach		60°
Angle of departure		40°
Seating capacity		4
Fording depth	800 mm	31½ ins.
Climbing ability		30°
Overturn gradient (lengthwise)		50°
Overturn gradient (crosswise)		30°
Turning radius	17 meters	55 ft., 2 ins.
Trailer load	3,500 kg	7,716 lb.
Engine horsepower	85 c—v	83.8 hp
Piston displacement	6,234 cu. cm.	374 cu. ins.
Fuel tank capacity	120 liters	31.7 gal.
Highway fuel consumption		7.3 m.p.g.
Average terrain fuel consumption		5.2 m.p.g.

German nomenclature: Verstärkerkraftwagen (Kfz. 61) mit Einheitsfahrgestell für leichter Lastkraftwagen.

English designation: Maintenance truck with standard chassis for light truck.

MOBILE PRINTING PRESS
Druck. Kw. (Kfz. 62)

Net weight	3,900 kg	8,597 lb.
Pay load	1,150 kg	2,535 lb.
Gross weight	5,050 kg	11,133 lb.
Weight: Front axle	1,350 kg	2,975 lb.
Weight: Rear axle, each	1,850 kg	4,078 lb.
Length (overall)	5,750 mm	18 ft., 10 ins.
Width (overall)	2,100 mm	6 ft., 10 ins.
Height (overall)	2,650 mm	8 ft., 8 ins.
Ground clearance	225 mm	8⅞ ins.
Tread centers	1,600 mm	5 ft., 3 ins.
	1,800 mm	5 ft., 11 ins.
	1,800 mm	5 ft., 11 ins.
Wheelbase	3,000/950 mm	118/37 ins.
Wheel width	170–350 mm	6¾/13¾ ins.
Angle of approach		60°
Angle of departure		40°
Seating capacity		3
Fording depth	600 mm	23⅝ ins.
Climbing ability		20°
Overturn gradient (lengthwise)		50°
Overturn gradient (crosswise)		30°
Turning radius	19.5 meters	64 ft.
Trailer load		
Engine horsepower	65 c–v	64.1 hp
Piston displacement	3,500 cu cm	210 cu. ins.
Fuel tank capacity	110 liters	29 gal.
Highway fuel consumption		5.9 m.p.g.
Average terrain fuel consumption		4.3 m.p.g.

German nomenclature: Druckereikraftwagen (Kfz. 62) mit Fahrgestell des leichter geländegängiger Lastkraftwagen (o).

English designation: Mobile printing press with special chassis for light cross-country truck.

FLASH RANGING TRUCK
Lichtausw. Kw. (Kfz. 62)

Net weight	3,900 kg	8,597 lb.
Pay load	1,150 kg	2,535 lb.
Gross weight	5,050 kg	11,133 lb.
Weight: Front axle	1,350 kg	2,975 lb.
Weight: Rear axle, each	1,850 kg	4,078 lb.
Length (overall)	5,750 mm	18 ft., 10 ins.
Width (overall)	2,100 mm	6 ft., 10 ins.
Height (overall)	2,650 mm	8 ft., 8 ins.
Ground clearance	225 mm	9⅞ ins.
Tread centers	1,600 mm	5 ft., 3 ins.
	1,800 mm	5 ft., 11 ins.
	1,800 mm	5 ft., 11 ins.
Wheelbase	3,000/950 mm	118/37 ins.
Wheel width	170–350 mm	6¾/13¾ ins.
Angle of approach		60°
Angle of departure		40°
Seating capacity		7
Fording depth	600 mm	23⅝ ins.
Climbing ability		20°
Overturn gradient (lengthwise)		50°
Overturn gradient (crosswise)		30°
Turning radius	19.5 meters	64 ft.
Trailer load		
Engine horsepower	65 c–v	64.1 hp
Piston displacement	3,900 cu cm	234 cu. ins.
Fuel tank capacity	110 liters	29 gal.
Highway fuel consumption		5.9 m.p.g.
Average terrain fuel consumption		4.3 m.p.g.

German nomenclature: Lichtauswerte-Kraftwagen (Kfz. 62) mit Fahrgestell des leichter geländegängiger Lastkraftwagen (o).

English designation: Flash ranging truck with special chassis for light cross-country truck.

49

SOUND DETECTOR TRUCK
Schallausn. Kw. (Kfz. 62)

GERMAN

German nomenclature. Schallausnahme - Kraftwagen (Kfz. 62) mit Fahrgestell des leichter geländegängiger Lastkraftwagen (o).

English designation: Sound detector truck with special chassis for light cross-country truck.

Net weight	3,900 kg	8,597 lb.
Pay load	1,150 kg	2,535 lb.
Gross weight	5,050 kg	11,133 lb.
Weight: Front axle	1,350 kg	2,975 lb.
Weight: Rear axle, each	1,850 kg	4,078 lb.
Length (overall)	5,750 mm	18 ft., 10 ins.
Width (overall)	2,100 mm	6 ft., 10 ins.
Height (overall)	2,650 mm	8 ft., 8 ins.
Ground clearance	225 mm	8⅞ ins.
Tread centers	1,600 mm	5 ft., 3 ins.
	1,800 mm	5 ft., 11 ins.
	1,800 mm	5 ft., 11 ins.
Wheelbase	3,000/950 mm	118/37 ins.
Wheel width	170–350 mm	6¾–13⅜ ins.
Angle of approach		50°
Angle of departure		35°
Seating capacity		7
Fording depth	600 mm	23⅝ ins.
Climbing ability		20°
Overturn gradient (lengthwise)		50°
Overturn gradient (crosswise)		30°
Turning radius	19.5 meters	64 ft.
Trailer load		
Engine horsepower	65 c–v	64.1 hp
Piston displacement	3,500 cu cm	210 cu. ins.
Fuel tank capacity	110 liters	29 gal.
Highway fuel consumption		5.9 m.p.g.
Average terrain fuel consumption		4.3 m.p.g.

SOUND PLOTTING TRUCK
Schallausw. Kw. — Verm. Ausw. Kw. — Stbs. Ausw. Kw. (Kfz. 62)

German nomenclature: Schallauswerte - Kraftwagen (Kfz. 62).
Vermessungsauswerte-Kraftwagen (Kfz. 62)
Stabsauswerte-Kraftwagen (Kfz. 62) mit Fahrgestell des leichter geländegängiger Lastkraftwagen (o).

English designation: Sound plotting truck.
Survey truck.
Command vehicle with special chassis for light cross-country truck.

Net weight	3,900 kg	8,597 lb.
Pay load	1,150 kg	2,535 lb.
Gross weight	5,050 kg	11,133 lb.
Weight: Front axle	1,350 kg	2,975 lb.
Weight: Rear axle, each	1,850 kg	4,078 lb.
Length (overall)	5,750 mm	18 ft., 10 ins.
Width (overall)	2,100 mm	6 ft., 10 ins.
Height (overall)	2,650 mm	8 ft., 8 ins.
Ground clearance	225 mm	8⅞ ins.
Tread centers	1,600 mm	5 ft., 3 ins.
	1,800 mm	5 ft., 11 ins.
	1,800 mm	5 ft., 11 ins.
Wheelbase	3,000/950 mm	118/37 ins.
Wheel width	170–350 mm	6¾–13¾ ins.
Angle of approach		60°
Angle of departure		40°
Seating capacity		7
Fording depth	600 mm	23⅝ ins.
Climbing ability		20°
Overturn gradient (lengthwise)		50°
Overturn gradient (crosswise)		30°
Turning radius	19.5 meters	64 ft.
Trailer load		
Engine horsepower	65 c–v	64.1 hp
Piston displacement	3,500 cu cm	210 cu. ins.
Fuel tank capacity	110 liters	29 gal.
Highway fuel consumption		5.9 m.p.g.
Average terrain fuel consumption		4.3 m.p.g.

METEOROLOGICAL TRUCK
Wett. Kw. (Kfz. 62)

Net weight	3,900 kg	8,597 lb.
Pay load	1,150 kg	2,535 lb.
Gross weight	5,050 kg	11,133 lb.
Weight: Front axle	1,350 kg	2,975 lb.
Weight: Rear axle, each	1,850 kg	4,078 lb.
Length (overall)	5,750 mm	18 ft., 10 ins.
Width (overall)	2,100 mm	6 ft., 10 ins.
Height (overall)	2,650 mm	8 ft., 8 ins.
Ground clearance	225 mm	8⅞ ins.
Tread centers	1,600 mm	5 ft., 3 ins.
	1,800 mm	5 ft., 11 ins.
	1,800 mm	5 ft., 11 ins.
Wheelbase	3,000/950 mm	118/37 ins.
Wheel width	170–350 mm	6¾–13¾ ins.
Angle of approach		60°
Angle of departure		40°
Seating capacity		
Fording depth	600 mm	23⅝ ins.
Climbing ability		20°
Overturn gradient (lengthwise)		50°
Overturn gradient (crosswise)		30°
Turning radius	19.5 meters	64 ft.
Trailer load		
Engine horsepower	65 c–v	64.1 hp
Piston displacement	3,500 cu cm	210 cu. ins.
Fuel tank capacity	110 liters	29 gal.
Highway fuel consumption		5.9 m.p.g.
Average terrain fuel consumption		4.3 m.p.g.

German nomenclature: Wetterkraftwagen (Kfz. 62) mit Fahrgestell des leichter geländegängiger Lastkraftwagen (o)

English designation: Meteorological truck with special chassis for light cross-country truck.

FLASH RANGING STATION TRUCK
Lichtm. St. Kw. — Schallm. St. Kw. — Vorw. Kw. — Schallm. Ger. Kw. (Kfz. 63)

Net weight	3,900 kg	8,597 lb.
Pay load	1,150 kg	2,535 lb.
Gross weight	5,050 kg	11,133 lb.
Weight: Front axle	1,300 kg	2,866 lb.
Weight: Rear axle, each	1,875 kg	4,133 lb.
Length (overall)	5,750 mm	18 ft., 10 ins.
Width (overall)	2,100 mm	6 ft., 10 ins.
Height (overall)	2,350 mm	7 ft., 8 ins.
Ground clearance	200 mm	7⅞ ins.
Tread centers	1,600 mm	5 ft., 3 ins.
	1,800 mm	5 ft., 11 ins.
	1,800 mm	5 ft., 11 ins.
Wheelbase	3,000/950 mm	118/37 ins.
Wheel width	170 mm	6¾ ins.
Angle of approach		60°
Angle of departure		40°
Seating capacity		7
Fording depth	600 mm	23⅝ ins.
Climbing ability		20°
Overturn gradient (lengthwise)		50°
Overturn gradient (crosswise)		30°
Turning radius	19.5 meters	64 ft.
Trailer load		
Engine horsepower		
Piston displacement		
Fuel tank capacity	110 liters	29 gal.
Highway fuel consumption		5.9 m.p.g.
Average terrain fuel consumption		4.3 m.p.g.

German nomenclature: Lichtmessstellenkraftwagen (Kfz. 63).
Schallmessstellenkraftwagen (Kfz. 63).
Vorwarnerkraftwagen (Kfz. 63).
Schallmessgerätkraftwagen (Kfz. 63) mit Fahrgestell des leichter geländegängiger Lastkraftwagen (o).

English designation: Flash ranging station truck.
Sound ranging truck.
Detector truck.
Sound predictor truck with special chassis for light cross-country truck.

RANGE FINDER TRUCK
Verm. Ger. Kw. (Kfz. 64)

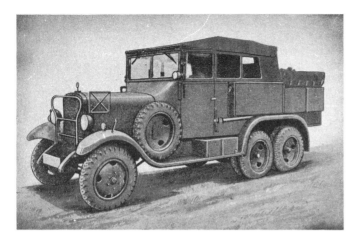

German nomenclature: Vermessungsgerätkraftwagen (Kfz. 64) mit Fahrgestell des leichter geländegängiger Lastkraftwagen (o).

English designation: Range finder truck with special chassis for light cross-country truck.

Net weight	3,900 kg	8,597 lb.
Pay load	1,150 kg	2,535 lb.
Gross weight	5,050 kg	11,133 lb.
Weight: Front axle	1,300 kg	2,866 lb.
Weight: Rear axle, each	1,875 kg	4,133 lb.
Length (overall)	5,750 mm	18 ft., 10 ins.
Width (overall)	2,150 mm	7 ft.
Height (overall)	2,350 mm	7 ft., 8 ins.
Ground clearance	200 mm	7⅞ ins.
Tread centers	1,600 mm	5 ft., 3 ins.
	1,800 mm	5 ft., 11 ins.
	1,800 mm	5 ft., 11 ins.
Wheelbase	3,000/950 mm	118/37 ins.
Wheel width	170 mm	6¾ ins.
Angle of approach		60°
Angle of departure		40°
Seating capacity		7
Fording depth	600 mm	23⅝ ins.
Climbing ability		20°
Overturn gradient (lengthwise)		50°
Overturn gradient (crosswise)		30°
Turning radius	19.5 meters	64 ft.
Trailer load		
Engine horsepower	65 c–v	64.1 hp
Piston displacement	3,500 cu cm	210 cu. ins.
Fuel tank capacity	110 liters	29 gal.
Highway fuel consumption		5.9 m.p.g.
Average terrain fuel consumption		4.3 m.p.g.

MEASUREMENT RANGE AND EQUIPMENT TRUCK
Messt.-u. Ger. Kw. (Kfz. 63)

German nomenclature: Messtellen-und Gerätkraftwagen (Kfz. 63) mit Einheitsfahrgestell für leichter Lastkraftwagen.

English designation: Measurement range and equipment truck with standard chassis for light truck.

Net weight	5,400 kg	11,904 lb.
Pay load	1,900 kg	4,188 lb.
Gross weight	7,300 kg	16,093 lb.
Weight: Front axle	2,200 kg	4,850 lb.
Weight: Rear axle, each	2,550 kg	5,622 lb.
Length (overall)	6,110 mm	20 ft.
Width (overall)	2,235 mm	7 ft., 4 ins.
Height (overall)	2,485 mm	8 ft., 2 ins.
Ground clearance	280 mm	11¼ ins.
Tread centers	1,720 mm	5 ft., 8 ins.
Wheelbase	3,100/1,100 mm	122/43 ins.
Wheel width	2.15 mm	8½ ins.
Angle of approach		60°
Angle of departure		40°
Seating capacity		7
Fording depth	800 mm	31½ ins.
Climbing ability		30°
Overturn gradient (lengthwise)		50°
Overturn gradient (crosswise)		30°
Turning radius	17 meters	55 ft., 2 ins.
Trailer load		
Engine horsepower	85 c–v	83.8 hp
Piston displacement	6,234 cu cm	374 cu. ins.
Fuel tank capacity	120 liters	31.7 gal.
Highway fuel consumption		7.3 m.p.g.
Average terrain fuel consumption		5.2 m.p.g.

MEDIUM MOTOR TRUCK, OPEN

m. Lkw. off. (o) — Pi. Kw. II — Wffm. Werkst. Kw. — Wffm. Ger. Kw.

German nomenclature: mittlerer Lastkraftwagen, offen (o).
Pionierkraftwagen II (mittlerer Lkw. (o)).
Waffenmeister-Werkstattkraftwagen (mittlerer Lkw. (o)).
Waffenmeister-Gerätkraftwagen (mittlerer Lkw. (o)).
English designation: Medium motor truck, open.
Engineers' truck.
Armorer's workshop truck.
Armorer's store truck (medium truck—standard commercial vehicle).

Net weight	4,500 kg	9,921 lb.
Pay load	3,500 kg	7,716 lb.
Gross weight	8,000 kg	17,636 lb.
Weight: Front axle	3,100 kg	6,834 lb.
Weight: Rear axle	4,900 kg	10,802 lb.
Length (overall)	7,200 mm	23 ft., 7 ins.
Width (overall)	2,500 mm	8 ft., 2 ins.
Height (overall)	2,600 mm	8 ft., 6 ins.
Ground clearance	200 mm	7⅞ ins.
Tread centers	1,700 mm	5 ft., 7 ins.
	2,000 mm	6 ft., 6 ins.
Wheelbase	5,300 mm	208 ins.
Wheel width	190 mm	7½ ins.
Angle of approach		60°
Angle of departure		40°
Seating capacity		35
Fording depth	500 mm	20 ins.
Climbing ability		15°
Overturn gradient (lengthwise)		40°
Overturn gradient (crosswise)		30°
Turning radius	20 meters	65 ft., 7 ins.
Trailer load	2,000 kg	4,409 lb.
Engine horsepower	70 c–v	69 hp
Piston displacement	4,500 cu cm	270 cu. ins.
Fuel tank capacity	120–120 liters	31.7–31.7 gal.
Highway fuel consumption		8.4 m.p.g.
Average terrain fuel consumption		

MEDIUM MOTOR TRUCK (CLOSED)

m. Lkw. (o) mit geschl. Einh. Aufbau (Kfz. 305²)

German nomenclature: mittlerer Lastkraftwagen (o), mit geschlossenem Einheitsaufbau (Kraftfahrzeug 305²).

English designation: Medium motor truck (standard commercial vehicle).

Net weight	4,000 kg	8,818 lb.
Pay load	1,700 kg	3,747 lb.
Gross weight	5,700 kg	12,566 lb.
Weight: Front axle	1,500 kg	3,307 lb.
Weight: Rear axle	4,200 kg	9,258 lb.
Length (overall)	5,600 mm	18 ft., 4 ins.
Width (overall)	2,150 mm	7 ft.
Height (overall)	2,850 mm	9 ft., 4 ins.
Ground clearance	200 mm	7⅞ ins.
Tread centers	1,542 mm	5 ft.
	1,620 mm	5 ft., 3 ins.
Wheelbase		
Wheel width	190 mm	7½ ins.
Angle of approach		60°
Angle of departure		30°
Seating capacity		20
Fording depth	500 mm	19⅞ ins.
Climbing ability		15°
Overturn gradient (lengthwise)		40°
Overturn gradient (crosswise)		30°
Turning radius	15 meters	49 ft., 2 ins.
Trailer load	2,000 kg	4,409 lb.
Engine horsepower	75 c–v	73.9 hp
Piston displacement	3,626 cu cm	217.6 cu. ins.
Fuel tank capacity	821 liters	216.8 gal.
Highway fuel consumption		9.4 m.p.g.
Average terrain fuel consumption		7.3 m.p.g.

TELEPHONE CONSTRUCTION TRUCK
Fsp. Baukw.

German nomenclature: Fernsprechbaukraftwagen (mittleren Lastkraftwagen offen (o)).

English designation: Telephone construction truck (medium motor truck open—standard commercial chassis).

Net weight	4,000 kg	8,818 lb.
Pay load	2,300 kg	5,071 lb.
Gross weight	6,300 kg	13,888 lb.
Weight: Front axle	2,000 kg	4,409 lb.
Weight: Rear axle	4,300 kg	9,480 lb.
Length (overall)	8,000 mm	26 ft., 3 ins.
Width (overall)	2,500 mm	8 ft., 2 ins.
Height (overall)	2,600 mm	8 ft., 6 ins.
Ground clearance	200 mm	7⅞ ins.
Tread centers	1,700 mm	5 ft., 7 ins.
	2,000 mm	6 ft., 7 ins.
Wheelbase	5,300 mm	208 ins.
Wheel width	190 mm	7½ ins.
Angle of approach		60°
Angle of departure		40°
Seating capacity		9
Fording depth	500 mm	20 ins.
Climbing ability		15°
Overturn gradient (lengthwise)		40°
Overturn gradient (crosswise)		30°
Turning radius	20 meters	65 ft., 7 ins.
Trailer load	2,000 kg	4,409 lb.
Engine horsepower	70 c–v	69 hp
Piston displacement	4,500 cu cm	270 cu. ins.
Fuel tank capacity	120–120 liters	31.7–31.7 gal.
Highway fuel consumption		6.7–8.4 m.p.g.
Average terrain fuel consumption		

CHARGING TRUCK
Samml. Kw. (Kfz. 42)

German nomenclature: Sammlerkraftwagen (Kfz. 42) mit Fahrgestell des mittlerer Lastkraftwagen (o).

English designation: Charging truck with special chassis for medium truck.

Net weight	3,800 kg	8,377 lb.
Pay load	2,050 kg	4,519 lb.
Gross weight	5,850 kg	12,896 lb.
Weight: Front axle	1,900 kg	4,188 lb.
Weight: Rear axle, each	3,950 kg	8,707 lb.
Length (overall)	6,950 mm	22 ft., 7 ins.
Width (overall)	2,300 mm	7 ft., 6 ins.
Height (overall)	2,840 mm	9 ft., 3 ins.
Ground clearance	200 mm	7⅞ ins.
Tread centers	1,700 mm	5 ft., 7 ins.
	2,000 mm	6 ft., 7 ins.
Wheelbase	4,000 mm	157 ins.
Wheel width	190 mm	7½ ins.
Angle of approach		60°
Angle of departure		40°
Seating capacity		3
Fording depth	500 mm	20 ins.
Climbing ability		15°
Overturn gradient (lengthwise)		40°
Overturn gradient (crosswise)		30°
Turning radius	20 meters	65 ft., 7 ins.
Trailer load	2,000 kg	4,409 lb.
Engine horsepower	70 c–v	69 hp
Piston displacement	3,800 cu cm	228 cu. ins.
Fuel tank capacity	120–120 liters	31.7–31.7 gal.
Highway fuel consumption		6.7–8.4 m.p.g.
Average terrain fuel consumption		

MEDIUM CROSS-COUNTRY TRUCK, OPEN

m. gl. Lkw., off. (o) — s. Fsp. Kw. — m. Scheinw. Kw. — Pi. Kw. I

German nomenclature: mittlerer geländegängiger Lastkraftwagen offen (o).
Schwerer Fernsprechkraftwagen.
Mittlerer Scheinwerferkraftwagen.
Pionierkraftwagen I (m. gl. Lkw. (o)).
English designation: Medium cross-country truck, open (standard commercial vehicle).
Heavy telephone truck.
Medium searchlight truck.
Engineers' truck.
(medium cross-country truck).

Net weight	6,000 kg	13,227 lb.
Pay load	2,500 kg	5,512 lb.
Gross weight	8,500 kg	18,739 lb.
Weight: Front axle	2,000 kg	4,409 lb.
Weight: Rear axle, each	3,250 kg	7,165 lb.
Length (overall)	7,400 mm	24 ft., 3 ins.
Width (overall)	2,500 mm	8 ft., 2 ins.
Height (overall)	3,200 mm	10 ft., 6 ins.
Ground clearance	200 mm	7⅞ ins.
Tread centers	1,750 mm	5 ft., 9 ins.
	3,250 mm	10 ft., 8 ins.
	3,250 mm	10 ft., 8 ins.
Wheelbase	3,750–1,100 mm	148/43¼ ins.
Wheel width	190 mm	7½ ins.
Angle of approach		45°
Angle of departure		30°
Seating capacity		28
Fording depth	600 mm	23⅝ ins.
Climbing ability		18°
Overturn gradient (lengthwise)		50°
Overturn gradient (crosswise)		30°
Turning radius	23 meters	75 ft., 5½ ins.
Trailer load	2,500 kg	5,512 lb.
Engine horsepower	110 c–v	108.5 hp
Piston displacement	6,000 cu cm	360 cu. ins.
Fuel tank capacity	120–120 liters	31.7 gal.
Highway fuel consumption		5.9–7.8 m.p.g.
Average terrain fuel consumption		3.9–5.2 m.p.g.

FLASH RANGING TRUCK

Lichtm. Ger. Kw.

German nomenclature: Lichtmessgerätkraftwagen (mittleren geländegängiger Lastkraftwagen (o)).

English designation: Flash ranging truck (medium cross-country motor truck) (standard commercial chassis).

Net weight	6,000 kg	13,227 lb.
Pay load	2,000 kg	4,409 lb.
Gross weight	8,000 kg	17,636 lb.
Weight: Front axle	2,200 kg	4,850 lb.
Weight: Rear axle, each	2,900 kg	6,393 lb.
Length (overall)	7,400 mm	24 ft., 3 ins.
Width (overall)	2,500 mm	8 ft., 2 ins.
Height (overall)	3,200 mm	10 ft., 6 ins.
Ground clearance	300 mm	11⅞ ins.
Tread centers	1,750 mm	5 ft., 9 ins.
	2,000 mm	6 ft., 7 ins.
	2,000 mm	6 ft., 7 ins.
Wheelbase	3,750/1,100 mm	148/43 ins.
Wheel width	190 mm	7½ ins.
Angle of approach		45°
Angle of departure		30°
Seating capacity		5
Fording depth	600 mm	23⅝ ins.
Climbing ability		18°
Overturn gradient (lengthwise)		50°
Overturn gradient (crosswise)		30°
Turning radius	23 meters	75 ft., 5 ins.
Trailer load	2,500 kg	5,512 lb.
Engine horsepower	100 c–v	98.6 hp
Piston displacement	6,000 cu cm	360 cu. ins.
Fuel tank capacity	120–120 liters	31.7 gal.
Highway fuel consumption		5.9–4.7 m.p.g.
Average terrain fuel consumption		3.9–5.2 m.p.g.

FIELD TELEPHONE CABLE TRUCK
Ft. Kabel Kw.

German nomenclature: Feldfernkabelkraftwagen (mittlerer geländegängig Lastkraftwagen offen (o)).

English designation: Field telephone cable truck (medium cross-country motor truck) open (standard commercial chassis).

Net weight	6,000 kg	13,227 lb.
Pay load	3,120 kg	6,878 lb.
Gross weight	9,120 kg	20,104 lb.
Weight: Front axle	2,210 kg	4,872 lb.
Weight: Rear axle, each	3,455 kg	7,616 lb.
Length (overall)	7,200 mm	23 ft., 7 ins.
Width (overall)	2,380 mm	11 ft., 9 ins.
Height (overall)	2,800 mm	9 ft., 2 ins.
Ground clearance	200 mm	7⅞ ins.
Tread centers	1,800 mm	5 ft., 11 ins.
	2,150 mm	7 ft.
	2,150 mm	7 ft.
Wheelbase	3,750/1,100 mm	148/43 ins.
Wheel width	190 mm	7½ ins.
Angle of approach		45°
Angle of departure		30°
Seating capacity		7
Fording depth	600 mm	23⅝ ins.
Climbing ability		18°
Overturn gradient (lengthwise)		50°
Overturn gradient (crosswise)		30°
Turning radius	23 meters	75 ft., 5 ins.
Trailer load	2,500 kg	5,512 lb.
Engine horsepower	100 c–v	98.6 hp
Piston displacement	6,000 cu cm	360 cu. ins.
Fuel tank capacity	120–120 liters	31.7 gal.
Highway fuel consumption		
Average terrain fuel consumption		

ANTIAIRCRAFT SURVEY SECTION TRUCK
Flak-Messtr. Kw. I und II (Kfz. 74)

German nomenclature: Flakmesstruppkraftwagen I (Kfz. 74).
Flakmesstruppkraftwagen II (Kfz. 74); mit Fahrgestell des mittleren geländegängiger Lastkraftwagen (o).

English designation: Antiaircraft survey section truck with special chassis for medium cross-country truck.

Net weight	6,000 kg	13,227 lb.
Pay load	2,200 kg	4,850 lb.
Gross weight	8,200 kg	18,377 lb.
Weight: Front axle	1,900 kg	4,188 lb.
Weight: Rear axle, each	3,150 kg	6,945 lb.
Length (overall)		
Width (overall)		
Height (overall)		
Ground clearance	200 mm	7⅞ ins.
Tread centers	1,750 mm	5 ft., 8 ins.
	2,000 mm	6 ft., 6 ins.
	2,000 mm	6 ft., 6 ins.
Wheelbase		
Wheel width	190 mm	7½ ins.
Angle of approach		45°
Angle of departure		30°
Seating capacity		14
Fording depth	600 mm	23⅝ ins.
Climbing ability		18°
Overturn gradient (lengthwise)		50°
Overturn gradient (crosswise)		35°
Turning radius	23 meters	75 ft., 5 ins.
Trailer load	3,250 kg	7,165 lb.
Engine horsepower	110 c–v	108.5 hp
Piston displacement	6,000 cu cm	360 cu. ins.
Fuel tank capacity	120–120 liters	31.7 gal.
Highway fuel consumption		
Average terrain fuel consumption		

MEDIUM ANTIAIRCRAFT UNIT TRUCK

m. Flakkw.

Net weight	6,000 kg	13,227 lb.
Pay load	2,100 kg	4,630 lb.
Gross weight	8,100 kg	17,857 lb.
Weight: Front axle	1,850 kg	4,078 lb.
Weight: Rear axle, each	3,125 kg	6,889 lb.
Length (overall)	7,400 mm	24 ft., 3 ins.
Width (overall)	2,500 mm	8 ft., 2 ins.
Height (overall)	3,200 mm	10 ft., 6 ins.
Ground clearance	200 mm	7⅞ ins.
Tread centers	1,750 mm	5 ft., 9 ins.
	2,000 mm	6 ft., 7 ins.
	2,000 mm	6 ft., 7 ins.
Wheelbase	3,750/1,100 mm	148/43 ins.
Wheel width	190 mm	7½ ins.
Angle of approach		45°
Angle of departure		30°
Seating capacity		11
Fording depth	600 mm	23⅝ ins.
Climbing ability		18°
Overturn gradient (lengthwise)		50°
Overturn gradient (crosswise)		35°
Turning radius	23 meters	75 ft., 5 ins.
Trailer load	3,550 kg	7,826 lb.
Engine horsepower	110 c–v	108.5 hp
Piston displacement	6,000 cu cm	360 cu. ins.
Fuel tank capacity	120–120 liters	31.7 gal.
Highway fuel consumption		5.9–7.8 m.p.g.
Average terrain fuel consumption		3.9–5.2 m.p.g.

German nomenclature: mittlerer Flakkraftwagen (mittlerer geländegängiger Lastkraftwagen (o)).

English designation: Medium antiaircraft unit truck (medium cross-country motor truck (standard commercial chassis)).

PHOTOGRAPHIC TRUCK

Bildkw. (Kfz. 354)

Net weight	7,200 kg	15,873 lb.
Pay load	900 kg	1,984 lb.
Gross weight	8,100 kg	17,857 lb.
Weight: Front axle	2,000 kg	4,409 lb.
Weight: Rear axle, each	3,050 kg	6,724 lb.
Length (overall)		
Width (overall)		
Height (overall)		
Ground clearance	200 mm	7⅞ ins.
Tread centers	1,750 mm	5 ft., 9 ins.
	2,000 mm	6 ft., 7 ins.
	2,000 mm	6 ft., 7 ins.
Wheelbase	3,750/1,100 mm	148/43 ins.
Wheel width	190 mm	7½ ins.
Angle of approach		45°
Angle of departure		30°
Seating capacity		6
Fording depth	600 mm	23⅝ ins.
Climbing ability		18°
Overturn gradient (lengthwise)		60°
Overturn gradient (crosswise)		35°
Turning radius		
Trailer load		
Engine horsepower		
Piston displacement		
Fuel tank capacity	150 liters	39.6 gal.
Highway fuel consumption		8.4–7.8 m.p.g.
Average terrain fuel consumption		6.7–5.2 m.p.g.

German nomenclature: Bildkraftwagen (Kfz. 354) mit Fahrgestell des mittleren geländegängiger Lastkraftwagen (o).

English designation: Photographic truck with special chassis for medium cross-country truck.

TELEPHONE EXCHANGE TRUCK
Fsp. Betr. Kw. (Kfz. 72)

German nomenclature: Fernsprech-Betriebskraftwagen (Kfz. 72) mit Fahrgestell des mittleren geländegängiger Lastkraftwagen (o).

English designation: Telephone exchange truck with special chassis for medium cross-country truck.

Net weight	6,700 kg	14,770 lb.
Pay load	2,050 kg	4,519 lb.
Gross weight	8,750 kg	19,290 lb.
Weight: Front axle	2,700 kg	5,952 lb.
Weight: Rear axle, each	3,025 kg	6,689 lb.
Length (overall)	7,000 mm	23 ft.
Width (overall)	2,300 mm	7 ft., 6 ins.
Height (overall)	2,860 mm	9 ft., 4 ins.
Ground clearance	200 mm	7⅞ ins.
Tread centers	1,750 mm	5 ft., 9 ins.
	2,000 mm	6 ft., 7 ins.
	2,000 mm	6 ft., 7 ins.
Wheelbase	3,750/1,100 mm	148/43 ins.
Wheel width	190 mm	7½ ins.
Angle of approach		45°
Angle of departure		30°
Seating capacity		2
Fording depth	600 mm	23⅝ ins.
Climbing ability		18°
Overturn gradient (lengthwise)		50°
Overturn gradient (crosswise)		30°
Turning radius	23 meters	75 ft., 5 ins.
Trailer load	2,500 kg	5,512 lb.
Engine horsepower	100 c-v	98.6 hp
Piston displacement	4,500 cu cm	270 cu. ins.
Fuel tank capacity	120 liters	31.7 gal.
Highway fuel consumption		5.9–7.8 m.p.g.
Average terrain fuel consumption		4.7–5.9 m.p.g.

TELETYPE TRUCK
Fernschr. Kw. (Kfz. 72)

German nomenclature: Fernschreibkraftwagen (Kfz. 72) mit Fahrgestell des mittleren geländegängiger Lastkraftwagen (o).

English designation: Teletype truck with special chassis for medium cross-country motor truck.

Net weight	6,400 kg	14,109 lb.
Pay load	2,100 kg	4,630 lb.
Gross weight	8,500 kg	18,739 lb.
Weight: Front axle	2,600 kg	5,732 lb.
Weight: Rear axle, each	2,950 kg	6,503 lb.
Length (overall)	7,000 mm	22 ft., 4 ins.
Width (overall)	2,250 mm	7 ft., 4 ins.
Height (overall)	3,050 mm	10 ft.
Ground clearance	250 mm	9⅞ ins.
Tread centers	1,750 mm	5 ft., 9 ins.
	2,000 mm	6 ft., 7 ins.
	2,000 mm	6 ft., 7 ins.
Wheelbase	3,750/1,100 mm	148/43 ins.
Wheel width	190 mm	7½ ins.
Angle of approach		45°
Angle of departure		30°
Seating capacity		4
Fording depth	600 mm	23⅝ ins.
Climbing ability		18°
Overturn gradient (lengthwise)		50°
Overturn gradient (crosswise)		30°
Turning radius	23 meters	75 ft., 5 ins.
Trailer load	2,500 kg	5,512 lb.
Engine horsepower	100 c-v	98.6 hp
Piston displacement	6,000 cu cm	360 cu. ins.
Fuel tank capacity	120 liters	31.7 gal.
Highway fuel consumption		5.9–7.8 m.p.g.
Average terrain fuel consumption		4.7–5.9 m.p.g.

TELETYPE TRUCK

Ferschr. Kw. (Kfz. 72/1)

Net weight	6,400 kg	14,109 lb.
Pay load	2,100 kg	4,629 lb.
Gross weight	8,500 kg	18,739 lb.
Weight: Front axle	2,600 kg	5,732 lb.
Weight: Rear axle, each	2,950 kg	6,503 lb.
Length (overall)	7,000 mm	22 ft., 11 ins.
Width (overall)	2,250 mm	7 ft., 4 ins.
Height (overall)	3,050 mm	10 ft.
Ground clearance	200 mm	7⅞ ins.
Tread centers	1,750 mm	5 ft., 9 ins.
	2,000 mm	6 ft., 7 ins.
	2,000 mm	6 ft., 7 ins.
Wheelbase	3,750/1,100 mm	148/43 ins.
Wheel width	190 mm	7½ ins.
Angle of approach		45°
Angle of departure		30°
Seating capacity		8
Fording depth	600 mm	23⅝ ins.
Climbing ability		18°
Overturn gradient (lengthwise)		50°
Overturn gradient (crosswise)		30°
Turning radius	25 meters	75 ft., 5 ins.
Trailer load	2,500 kg	5,512 lb.
Engine horsepower	100 c–v	98.6 hp
Piston displacement	6,000 cu cm	360 cu. ins.
Fuel tank capacity	120 liters	31.7 gal.
Highway fuel consumption		5.9–7.8 m.p.g.
Average terrain fuel consumption		4.7–5.9 m.p.g.

German nomenclatutre: Fernschreibkraftwagen (Kfz. 72/1) mit Fahrgestell des mittleren geländegängiger Lastkraftwagen (o).

English designation: Teletype truck with special chassis for medium cross-country motor truck.

RADIO TELETYPE TRUCK

Fu. Betr. Kw. (Kfz. 72)

Net weight	5,950 kg	13,117 lb.
Pay load	2,150 kg	4,739 lb.
Gross weight	8,100 kg	17,857 lb.
Weight: Front axle	2,500 kg	5,512 lb.
Weight: Rear axle, each	2,800 kg	6,173 lb.
Length (overall)	7,000 mm	22 ft., 11 ins.
Width (overall)	2,200 mm	7 ft., 2 ins.
Height (overall)	2,750 mm	9 ft.
Ground clearance	300 mm	11⅞ ins.
Tread centers	1,750 mm	5 ft., 9 ins.
	2,000 mm	6 ft., 7 ins.
	2,000 mm	6 ft., 7 ins.
Wheelbase	3,750/1,100 mm	148/43 ins.
Wheel width	190 mm	7½ ins.
Angle of approach		45°
Angle of departure		30°
Seating capacity		10
Fording depth	600 mm	23⅝ ins.
Climbing ability		18°
Overturn gradient (lengthwise)		45°
Overturn gradient (crosswise)		30°
Turning radius	25 meters	75 ft., 5 ins.
Trailer load	2,000 kg	4,409 lb.
Engine horsepower	90 c–v	88.8 hp
Piston displacement	6,000 cu cm	360 cu. ins.
Fuel tank capacity	120 liters	31.7 gal.
Highway fuel consumption		5.9 m.p.g.
Average terrain fuel consumption		3.9 m.p.g.

German nomenclature: Funkbetriebskraftwagen (Kfz. 72) mit Fahrgestell des mittleren geländegängiger Lastkraftwagen (o).

English designation: Radio teletype truck with special chassis for medium cross-country motor truck.

RADIO TRUCK
Fu. Kw. a — Fu. Kw. b (Kfz. 72)

Net weight	5,950 kg	13,117 lb.
Pay load	2,500 kg	5,512 lb.
Gross weight	8,450 kg	18,628 lb.
Weight: Front axle	2,650 kg	5,842 lb.
Weight: Rear axle, each	2,900 kg	6,393 lb.
Length (overall)	7,100 mm	23 ft., 3 ins.
Width (overall)	2,500 mm	7 ft., 6 ins.
Height (overall)	2,800 mm	9 ft., 2 ins.
Ground clearance	300 mm	11⅞ ins.
Tread centers	1,750 mm	5 ft., 9 ins.
	2,000 mm	6 ft., 7 ins.
	2,000 mm	6 ft., 7 ins.
Wheelbase	3,750/1,100 mm	148/43 ins.
Wheel width	190 mm	7½ ins.
Angle of approach		45°
Angle of departure		30°
Seating capacity		3
Fording depth	600 mm	23⅝ ins.
Climbing ability		18°
Overturn gradient (lengthwise)		40°
Overturn gradient (crosswise)		30°
Turning radius	23 meters	75 ft., 5 ins.
Trailer load	2,000 kg	4,409 lb.
Engine horsepower	90 c–v	88.8 hp
Piston displacement	6,000 cu cm	360 cu. ins.
Fuel tank capacity	120 liters	31.7 gal.
Highway fuel consumption		5.9 m.p.g.
Average terrain fuel consumption		3.9 m.p.g.

German nomenclature: Funkkraftwagen a; Funkkraft-wagen b (Kfz. 72) mit Fahrgestell des mittleren geländegängiger Lastkraftwagen (o).

English designation: Radio trucks A and B with special chassis for medium cross-country motor truck.

RADIO INTERCEPTION TRUCK
Fu. Horchkw. a (Kfz. 72)

Net weight	5,695 kg	12,555 lb.
Pay load	2,175 kg	4,795 lb.
Gross weight	7,870 kg	17,349 lb.
Weight: Front axle	2,200 kg	4,850 lb.
Weight: Rear axle, each	2,835 kg	6,250 lb.
Length (overall)	7,000 mm	22 ft., 11 ins.
Width (overall)	2,835 mm	9 ft., 3 ins.
Height (overall)	5,900 mm	12 ft., 9 ins.
Ground clearance	300 mm	11⅞ ins.
Tread centers	1,800 mm (front)	5 ft., 11 ins.
	2,000 mm (rear)	6 ft., 7 ins.
Wheelbase	3,750/1,100 mm	148/43 ins.
Wheel width	190 mm	7½ ins.
Angle of approach		45°
Angle of departure		30°
Seating capacity		4
Fording depth	600 mm	23⅝ ins.
Climbing ability		18°
Overturn gradient (lengthwise)		40°
Overturn gradient (crosswise)		30°
Turning radius	23 meters	75 ft., 5 ins.
Trailer load	2,000 kg	4,409 lb.
Engine horsepower	100 c–v	98.6 hp
Piston displacement	6,000 cu cm	360 cu. ins.
Fuel tank capacity	120 liters	31.7 gal.
Highway fuel consumption		5.9–7.8 m.p.g.
Average terrain fuel consumption		4.7–5.9 m.p.g.

German nomenclature: Funkhorchkraftwagen a (Kfz. 72) mit Fahrgestell des mittleren geländegängiger Lastkraftwagen (o).

English designation: Radio interception truck A with special chassis for medium cross-country motor truck.

METEOROLOGICAL TRUCK
Vett. Kw. — Druck. Kw. (Kfz. 72)

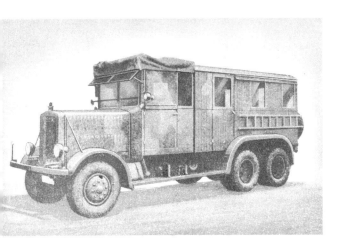

Net weight	6,000 kg	13,227 lb.
Pay load	3,000 kg	6,614 lb.
Gross weight	9,000 kg	19,840 lb.
Weight: Front axle	2,200 kg	4,850 lb.
Weight: Rear axle, each	3,400 kg	7,496 lb.
Length (overall)	7,100 mm	23 ft., 3 ins.
Width (overall)	2,300 mm	7 ft., 6 ins.
Height (overall)	2,800 mm	9 ft., 2 ins.
Ground clearance	330 mm	13 ins.
Tread centers	1,750 mm	5 ft., 9 ins.
	2,000 mm	6 ft., 7 ins.
	2,000 mm	6 ft., 7 ins.
Wheelbase	3,750/1,100 mm	148/43 ins.
Wheel width	190 mm	7½ ins.
Angle of approach		45°
Angle of departure		30°
Seating capacity		7
Fording depth		
Overturn gradient (lengthwise)		40°
Overturn gradient (crosswise)		30°
Climbing ability	600 mm	23⅝ ins.
Turning radius	23 meters	75 ft., 5 ins.
Trailer load		
Engine horsepower	90 c–v	88.8 hp
Piston displacement	6,000 cu cm	360 cu. ins.
Fuel tank capacity	120 liters	31.7 gal.
Highway fuel consumption		5.9 m.p.g.
Average terrain fuel consumption		3.9 m.p.g.

German nomenclature: Wetterkraftwagen (Kfz. 72).
Druckereikraftwagen (Kfz. 72) mit Fahrgestell des
mittleren geländegängiger Lastkraftwagen (o).

English designation: Meteorological truck.
Mobile printing truck with special chassis for
medium cross-country motor truck.

INTERCEPTOR TRUCK
Horch. Fu. Peil. Kw. (Kfz. 303)

Net weight	6,470 kg	14,263 lb.
Pay load	2,230 kg	4,916 lb.
Gross weight	8,700 kg	19,160 lb.
Weight: Front axle	2,200 kg	4,850 lb.
Weight: Rear axle, each	3,250 kg	7,165 lb.
Length (overall)	7,350 mm	24 ft., 1 in.
Width (overall)	2,500 mm	8 ft., 2 ins.
Height (overall)	2,950 mm	9 ft., 8 ins.
Ground clearance	200 mm	7⅞ ins.
Tread centers	1,750 mm	5 ft., 9 ins.
	2,000 mm	6 ft., 7 ins.
	2,000 mm	6 ft., 7 ins.
Wheelbase	3,750/1,100 mm	148/43 ins.
Wheel width	190 mm	7½ ins.
Angle of approach		45°
Angle of departure		30°
Seating capacity		6
Fording depth	600 mm	23⅝ ins.
Climbing ability		18°
Overturn gradient (lengthwise)		50°
Overturn gradient (crosswise)		30°
Turning radius		
Trailer load	3,500 kg	7,716 lb.
Engine horsepower	95 c–v	93.7 hp
Piston displacement	7,350 cu cm	441 cu. ins.
Fuel tank capacity	120 liters	31.7 gal.
Highway fuel consumption		5.9–7.8 m.p.g.
Average terrain fuel consumption		4.7–5.9 m.p.g.

German nomenclature: Horchfunkpeil-Kraftwagen (Kfz.
303) mit Fahrgestell des mittleren geländegängiger
Lastkraftwagen (o).

English designation: Interceptor truck with special
chassis for medium cross-country motor truck.

RADIO ANTENNA TRUCK

Fu. Mast. Kw. (Kfz. 301)

German nomenclature: Funkmast-Kraftwagen (Kfz. 301) mit Fahrgestell des mittleren geländegängiger Lastkraftwagen (o).

English designation: Radio antenna truck with special chassis for medium cross-country motor truck.

Net weight	6,300 kg	13,888 lb.
Pay load	1,850 kg	4,078 lb.
Gross weight	8,150 kg	17,967 lb.
Weight: Front axle	2,500 kg	5,512 lb.
Weight: Rear axle, each	2,825 kg	6,228 lb.
Length (overall)	7,550 mm	24 ft., 9 ins.
Width (overall)	2,350 mm	7 ft., 8 ins.
Height (overall)	2,750 mm	9 ft.
Ground clearance	250 mm	9⅞ ins.
Tread centers	1,750 mm	5 ft., 9 ins.
	2,000 mm	6 ft., 7 ins.
	2,000 mm	6 ft., 7 ins.
Wheelbase	3,750/1,100 mm	148/43 ins.
Wheel width	190 mm	7½ ins.
Angle of approach		45°
Angle of departure		30°
Seating capacity		5
Fording depth	600 mm	23⅝ ins.
Climbing ability		18°
Overturn gradient (lengthwise)		
Overturn gradient (crosswise)		
Turning radius	23 meters	75 ft., 5 ins.
Trailer load	2,000 kg	4,409 lb.
Engine horsepower	95 c–v	93.7 hp
Piston displacement	7,350 cu cm	441 cu. ins.
Fuel tank capacity	120 liters	31.7 gal.
Highway fuel consumption		7.8 m.p.g.
Average terrain fuel consumption		5.9 m.p.g.

HEAVY MOTOR TRUCK, OPEN

s. Lkw., Off. (o)

German nomenclature: schwerer Lastkraftwagen, offen (o).

English designation: Heavy motor truck, open (standard commercial vehicle).

Net weight	8,900 kg	19,620 lb.
Pay load	3,500 kg	7,716 lb.
Gross weight	18,500 kg	40,785 lb.
Weight: Front axle	6,500 kg	14,329 lb.
Weight: Rear axle, each	6,000 kg	13,227 lb.
Length (overall)	10,400 mm	34 ft., 1 in.
Width (overall)	2,500 mm	8 ft., 2 ins.
Height (overall)	2,600 mm	8 ft., 6 ins.
Ground clearance	250 mm	9⅞ ins.
Tread centers	200 mm	7⅞ ins.
Wheelbase	5,700/1,450 mm	224/57 ins.
Wheel width	230 mm	9 ins.
Angle of approach		55°
Angle of departure		50°
Seating capacity		40
Fording depth	600 mm	23⅝ ins.
Climbing ability		12°
Overturn gradient (lengthwise)		40°
Overturn gradient (crosswise)		30°
Turning radius	25 meters	82 ft.
Trailer load	5,000 kg	11,023 lb.
Engine horsepower	120 c/v	118.4 hp
Piston displacement	10,000 cu cm	600 cu. ins.
Fuel tank capacity	150–150 liters	39.6 gal.
Highway fuel consumption		4.7–6.7 m.p.g.
Average terrain fuel consumption		

IGHT MOTOR BUS

Kom. (o)

Net weight	2,500 kg	5,512 lb.
Pay load	1,500 kg	3,307 lb.
Gross weight	4,000 kg	8,818 lb.
Weight: Front axle	1,600 kg	3,527 lb.
Weight: Rear axle	2,400 kg	5,292 lb.
Length (overall)	6,000 mm	19 ft., 8 ins.
Width (overall)	1,750 mm	5 ft., 8 ins.
Height (overall)	2,000 mm	6 ft., 6 ins.
Ground clearance	200 mm	7⅞ ins.
Tread centers	1,420 mm	4 ft., 8 ins.
Wheelbase	3,900 mm	153 ins.
Wheel width	175 mm	6⅝ ins.
Angle of approach		40°
Angle of departure		20°
Seating capacity		15
Fording depth	500 mm	20 ins.
Climbing ability		12°
Overturn gradient (lengthwise)		50°
Overturn gradient (crosswise)		30°
Turning radius	16 meters	52 ft., 6 ins.
Trailer load		
Engine horsepower	50 c–v	49.3 hp
Piston displacement	3,000 cu cm	180 cu. ins.
Fuel tank capacity	120 liters	31.7 gal.
Highway fuel consumption		7.8–9.4 m.p.g.
Average terrain fuel consumption		

erman nomenclature: Leichter Kraftomnibus (o).

nglish designation: Light motor bus (standard commercial vehicle).

EDIUM MOTOR BUS

. Kom. (o) — Bef. Kw. — Fu. Answ. Kw. — Labor. Kw.

Net weight	4,300 kg	9,480 lb.
Pay load	3,000 kg	6,614 lb.
Gross weight	7,300 kg	16,093 lb.
Weight: Front axle	2,100 kg	4,630 lb.
Weight: Rear axle	5,200 kg	11,463 lb.
Length (overall)	7,300 mm	23 ft., 11 ins.
Width (overall)	2,100 mm	6 ft., 10 ins.
Height (overall)	3,000 mm	9 ft., 10 ins.
Ground clearance	200 mm	7⅞ ins.
Tread centers	1,750 mm	5 ft., 9 ins.
	1,910 mm	6 ft., 3 ins.
Wheelbase	4,400 mm	14 ft., 5 ins.
Wheel width	190 mm	7½ ins.
Angle of approach		40°
Angle of departure		20°
Seating capacity		30
Fording depth	500 mm	20 ins.
Climbing ability		12°
Overturn gradient (lengthwise)		40°
Overturn gradient (crosswise)		35°
Turning radius	20 meters	65 ft., 7 ins.
Trailer load	2,000 kg	4,409 lb.
Engine horsepower	90 c–v	88.8 hp
Piston displacement	9,000 cu cm	540 cu. ins.
Fuel tank capacity	120 liters	31.7 gal.
Highway fuel consumption		
Average terrain fuel consumption		5.9–7.8 m.p.g.

erman nomenclature: mittlerer Kraftomnibus (o) zugleich als; Befehlskraftwagen; Funkauswertekraftwagen; Laboratoriumskraftwagen.

nglish designation: Medium motor bus (standard commercial vehicle) used as Command Vehicle; Radio Intelligence Truck; Laboratory Truck.

HEAVY MOTOR BUS
s. Kom.

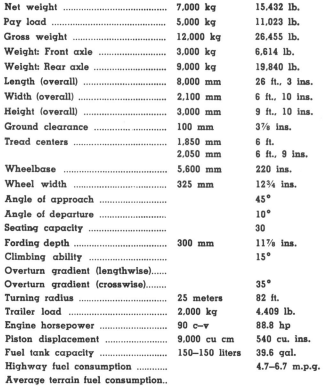

Net weight	7,000 kg	15,432 lb.
Pay load	5,000 kg	11,023 lb.
Gross weight	12,000 kg	26,455 lb.
Weight: Front axle	3,000 kg	6,614 lb.
Weight: Rear axle	9,000 kg	19,840 lb.
Length (overall)	8,000 mm	26 ft., 3 ins.
Width (overall)	2,100 mm	6 ft., 10 ins.
Height (overall)	3,000 mm	9 ft., 10 ins.
Ground clearance	100 mm	3⅞ ins.
Tread centers	1,850 mm	6 ft.
	2,050 mm	6 ft., 9 ins.
Wheelbase	5,600 mm	220 ins.
Wheel width	325 mm	12¾ ins.
Angle of approach		45°
Angle of departure		10°
Seating capacity		30
Fording depth	300 mm	11⅞ ins.
Climbing ability		15°
Overturn gradient (lengthwise)		
Overturn gradient (crosswise)		35°
Turning radius	25 meters	82 ft.
Trailer load	2,000 kg	4,409 lb.
Engine horsepower	90 c—v	88.8 hp
Piston displacement	9,000 cu cm	540 cu. ins.
Fuel tank capacity	150–150 liters	39.6 gal.
Highway fuel consumption		4.7–6.7 m.p.g.
Average terrain fuel consumption		

German nomenclature: schwerer Kraftomnibus (o).

English designation: Heavy motor bus (standard commercial vehicle).

SIGNAL REPAIR TRUCK
Nachr. Werkst. Kw. (Kfz. 42)

Net weight	4,400 kg	9,700 lb.
Pay load	2,200 kg	4,850 lb.
Gross weight	6,600 kg	14,550 lb.
Weight: Front axle	2,488 kg	5,486 lb.
Weight: Rear axle, each	4,112 kg	9,064 lb.
Length (overall)	6,950 mm	22 ft., 9 ins.
Width (overall)	2,300 mm	7 ft., 6 ins.
Height (overall)	2,840 mm	9 ft., 4 ins.
Ground clearance	200 mm	7⅞ ins.
Tread centers	1,700 mm	5 ft., 7 ins.
	2,000 mm	6 ft., 7 ins.
Wheelbase	4,000 mm	157 ins.
Wheel width	190 mm	7½ ins.
Angle of approach		60°
Angle of departure		40°
Seating capacity		3
Fording depth	500 mm	20 ins.
Climbing ability		15°
Overturn gradient (lengthwise)		40°
Overturn gradient (crosswise)		30°
Turning radius	20 meters	65 ft., 7 ins.
Trailer load	2,000 kg	4,409 lb.
Engine horsepower	70 c—v	69 hp
Piston displacement	4,530 cu cm	272 cu. ins.
Fuel tank capacity	120–120 liters	31.7 gal.
Highway fuel consumption		6.7–8.4 m.p.g.
Average terrain fuel consumption		

German nomenclature: Nachrichtenwerkstattkraftwagen (Kfz. 42) mit Fahrgestell des mittleren Lastkraftwagen (o).

English designation: Signal repair truck with special chassis for medium motor truck.

WORKSHOP TRUCK
Werkst. Kw. (Kfz. 51)

Net weight	6,500 kg	14,329 lb.
Pay load	6,500 kg	14,329 lb.
Gross weight	13,000 kg	28,656 lb.
Weight: Front axle	4,300 kg	9,430 lb.
Weight: Rear axle, each	8,700 kg	19,180 lb.
Length (overall)	8,000 mm	26 ft., 3 ins.
Width (overall)	2,350 mm	7 ft., 8 ins.
Height (overall)	3,000 mm	9 ft., 10 ins.
Ground clearance	200 mm	7⅞ ins.
Tread centers	1,850 mm	6 ft.
	2,050 mm	6 ft., 9 ins.
Wheelbase	5,100 mm	200 ins.
Wheel width	230 mm	9 ins.
Angle of approach		45°
Angle of departure		30°
Seating capacity		2
Fording depth	500 mm	20 ins.
Climbing ability		12°
Overturn gradient (lengthwise)		50°
Overturn gradient (crosswise)		30°
Turning radius	20 meters	65 ft., 7 ins.
Trailer load		
Engine horsepower	120 c–v	118.4 hp
Piston displacement	10,000 cu cm	600 cu. ins.
Fuel tank capacity	120 liters	31.7 gal.
Highway fuel consumption		5.2 m.p.g.
Average terrain fuel consumption..		

German nomenclature: Werkstattkraftwagen (Kfz. 51) mit Fahrgestell des schwerer Lastkraftwagen (o).

English designation: Workshop truck with special chassis for heavy motor truck.

WORKSHOP TRUCK
Werkst. Kw. (Kfz. 79)

Net weight	7,000 kg	15,432 lb.
Pay load		
Gross weight	9,800 to 10,700 kg	21,605 to 23,589 lb.
Weight: Front axle	2,200 to 2,800 kg	4,850 to 6,173 lb.
Weight: Rear axle, each	3,800 to 3,950 kg	8,377 to 8,707 lb.
Length (overall)	7,550 mm	24 ft., 10 ins.
Width (overall)	2,500 mm	8 ft., 2 ins.
Height (overall)	3,200 mm	10 ft., 6 ins.
Ground clearance	330 mm	13 ins.
Tread centers	1,750 mm	5 ft., 9 ins.
	2,000 mm	6 ft., 7 ins.
	2,000 mm	6 ft., 7 ins.
Wheelbase	3,750/1,100 mm	148–43 ins.
Wheel width	190/400 mm	7½–15¾ ins.
Angle of approach		45°
Angle of departure		30°
Seating capacity		2
Fording depth	600 mm	23⅝ ins.
Climbing ability		18°
Overturn gradient (lengthwise)		40°
Overturn gradient (crosswise)		30°
Turning radius	23 meters	75 ft., 5 ins.
Trailer load	2,000 kg	4,409 lb.
Engine horsepower	100 c–v	98.6 hp
Piston displacement	6,000 cu cm	360 cu. ins.
Fuel tank capacity	120–120 liters	31.7 gal.
Highway fuel consumption		5.9–7.8 m.p.g.
Average terrain fuel consumption..		3.9–5.2 m.p.g.

German nomenclature: Werkstattkraftwagen (Kfz. 79) mit Fahrgestell des mittleren geländegängiger Lastkraftwagen (o).

English designation: Workshop truck with special chassis for medium cross-country motor truck.

MEDIUM FUEL SERVICING TRUCK
m. Betr. St. Kess. Kw. (o)

German nomenclature: mittlerer Betriebstoffkessel-kraftwagen (o) mit Fahrgestell des mittleren Last-kraftwagen (o).

English designation: Medium fuel servicing truck with special chassis for medium motor truck (standard commercial vehicle).

Net weight	5,500 kg	12,125 lb.
Pay load	2,800 kg	6,173 lb.
Gross weight	8,300 kg	18,298 lb.
Weight: Front axle	2,600 kg	5,732 lb.
Weight: Rear axle	5,700 kg	12,566 lb.
Length (overall)	6,750 mm	22 ft., 1 in.
Width (overall)	2,250 mm	7 ft., 4 ins.
Height (overall)	2,600 mm	8 ft., 6 ins.
Ground clearance	240 mm	9½ ins.
Tread centers	1,600 mm	5 ft., 3 ins.
	1,880 mm	6 ft., 2 ins.
Wheelbase	4,500 mm	177 ins.
Wheel width	220/460 mm	8⅝/18⅛ ins.
Angle of approach		60°
Angle of departure		23°
Seating capacity		1
Fording depth	500 mm	20 ins.
Climbing ability		15°
Overturn gradient (lengthwise)		40°
Overturn gradient (crosswise)		25°
Turning radius	20 meters	65 ft., 7 ins.
Trailer load	2,000 kg	4,409 lb.
Engine horsepower	80 c—v	78.9 hp
Piston displacement	7,000 cu cm	420 cu. ins.
Fuel tank capacity	120 liters	31.7 gal.
Highway fuel consumption		6.7—8.4 m.p.g.
Average terrain fuel consumption		

HEAVY FUEL SERVICING TRUCK
s. Betr. St. Kess. Kw. (o)

German nomenclature: schwerer Betriebstoffkessel-kraftwagen (o) mit Fahrgestell des schwerer Last-kraftwagen (o).

English designation: Heavy fuel servicing truck with special chassis for heavy motor truck (standard com-mercial vehicle).

Net weight	8,000 kg	17,636 lb.
*Pay load	5,000 kg	11,023 lb.
Gross weight	13,000 kg	28,659 lb.
Weight: Front axle	5,000 kg	11,023 lb.
Weight: Rear axle	8,000 kg	17,636 lb.
Length (overall)	8,500 mm	27 ft., 10 ins.
Width (overall)	2,500 mm	8 ft., 2 ins.
Height (overall)	2,600 mm	8 ft., 6 ins.
Ground clearance	200 mm	7⅞ ins.
Tread centers	1,980 mm	6 ft., 6 ins.
	2,150 mm	7 ft.
Wheelbase	5,200 mm	204 ins.
Wheel width	320/680 mm	12½/26¾ ins.
Angle of approach		45°
Angle of departure		30°
Seating capacity		1
Fording depth	450 mm	17¾ ins.
Climbing ability		15°
Overturn gradient (lengthwise)		50°
Overturn gradient (crosswise)		30°
Turning radius	23 meters	75 ft., 5 ins.
Trailer load		
Engine horsepower	110 c—v	108.5 hp
Piston displacement	10,000 cu cm	600 cu. ins.
Fuel tank capacity	150—150 liters	39.6 gal.
Highway fuel consumption		5.9—7.8 m.p.g.
Average terrain fuel consumption		
*Cyl. of 6,500 l. cap		1,717 gal.

UEL SERVICING TRUCK

etr. St. Kesselkw. (Sd. Kfz. 5)

Net weight	6,270 kg	13,822 lb.
Pay load	2,930 kg	6,457 lb.
Gross weight	9,200 kg	20,280 lb.
Weight: Front axle	2,160 kg	4,761 lb.
Weight: Rear axle	3,520 kg each	7,760 lb. each
Length (overall)	7,350 mm	24 ft., 1 in.
Width (overall)	2,500 mm	8 ft., 2 ins.
Height (overall)	2,500 mm	8 ft., 2 ins.
Ground clearance	200 mm	7⅞ ins.
Tread centers	1,750 mm	5 ft., 9 ins.
	2,000 mm	6 ft., 7 ins.
Wheelbase	2,750/1,100 mm	108/43 ins.
Wheel width	190/400 mm	7½/15¾ ins.
Angle of approach		45°
Angle of departure		30°
Seating capacity		1
Fording depth	600 mm	23 ins.
Climbing ability		18°
Overturn gradient (lengthwise)		40°
Overturn gradient (crosswise)		30°
Turning radius	23 meters	75 ft., 5 ins.
Trailer load		
Engine horsepower	90 c–v	88.8 hp
Piston displacement	60,000 cu cm	3,600 cu. ins.
Fuel tank capacity	120/120 liters	31.7 gal.
Highway uel consumption		5.9/7.8 m.p.g.
Average terrain fuel consumption..		3.91/5.2 m.p.g.

German nomenclature: Betriebstoffkesselkraftwagen (Sd. Kfz. 5) mit Fahrgestell des mittleren gelädegängiger Lastkraftwagen (o).

glish designation: Fuel servicing truck with special chassis of the medium cross-country motor truck.

EROPLANE FUEL SERVICING TRUCK

ɔ. K. Kw. (Kfz. 384)

Net weight	6,300 kg	13,888 lb.
Pay load	2,625 kg	5,785 lb.
Gross weight	8,925 kg	19,675 lb.
Weight: Front axle	2,625 kg	5,785 lb.
Weight: Rear axle	3,150 kg each	6,945 lb. each
Length (overall)	7,230 mm	23 ft., 8 ins.
Width (overall)	2,500 mm	8 ft., 2 ins.
Height (overall)	2,450 mm	8 ft.
Ground clearance	200 mm	7⅞ ins.
Tread centers	1,750 mm	5 ft., 9 ins.
	2,000 mm	6 ft., 7 ins.
Wheelbase	3,750/1,100 mm	148/43 ins.
Wheel width	190/400 mm	7½/15¾ ins.
Angle of approach		50°
Angle of departure		30°
Seating capacity		1
Fording depth	600 mm	23 ins.
Climbing ability		18°
Overturn gradient (lengthwise)		50°
Overturn gradient (crosswise)		40°
Turning radius	17.5 meters	57 ft., 5 ins.
Trailer load	3,500 kg	7,716 lb.
Engine horsepower	95 c–v	93.7 hp
Piston displacement	7,350 cu cm	441 cu. ins.
Fuel tank capacity	122 liters	34.9 gal.
Highway fuel consumption		6.5 m.p.g.
Average terrain fuel consumption..	5.6 m.p.g.	

German nomenclature: Flugbetriebestoffkesselkraftwagen (Kfz. 384) mit Fahrgestell des mittleren geländegängiger Lastkraftwagen (o).

glish designation: Aeroplane fuel servicing truck with special chassis of the medium cross-country motor truck.

FIRE EXTINGUISHER TRUCK
Ls. Kw. (Kfz. 345)

German nomenclature: Löschkraftwagen (Kfz. 345) mit Fahrgestell des leichter Lastkraftwagen (o).

English designation: Fire extinguisher truck with special chassis of the light motor truck.

Net weight	2,615 kg	5,763 lb.
Pay load	670 kg	1,479 lb.
Gross weight	3,285 kg	7,242 lb.
Weight: Front axle	1,015 kg	2,238 lb.
Weight: Rear axle	2,270 kg	5,004 lb.
Length (overall)	5,250 mm	17 ft., 3 ins.
Width (overall)	2,050 mm	6 ft., 9 ins.
Height (overall)	2,300 mm	7 ft., 6 ins.
Ground clearance	205 mm	8 ins.
Tread centers	1,340 mm	4 ft., 4 ins.
	1,360 mm	4 ft., 5 ins.
Wheelbase	3,250 mm	128 ins.
Wheel width	170/350 mm	6¾/13¾ ins.
Angle of approach		40°
Angle of departure		16°
Seating capacity		9
Fording depth		
Climbing ability		15°
Overturn gradient (lengthwise)		50°
Overturn gradient (crosswise)		40°
Turning radius	14 meters	46 ft., 4 ins.
Trailer load	1,000 kg	2,205 lb.
Engine horsepower	55 c–v	54.2 hp
Piston displacement	2,473 cu cm	265 cu. ins.
Fuel tank capacity	50 liters	13.2 gal.
Highway fuel consumption		11.7 m.p.g.
Average terrain fuel consumption..		9.4 m.p.g.

FIRE ENGINE
Fl. Ks. 15 (o)

German nomenclature: Kraftfahrspritze (o) mit Fahrgestell des mittleren Lastkraftwagen (o).

English designation: Fire engine with special chassis of the medium motor truck (standard commercial vehicle).

Net weight	4,700 kg	10,361 lb.
Pay load	7,400 kg	5,292 lb.
Gross weight	7,100 kg	15,652 lb.
Weight: Front axle	2,300 kg	5,071 lb.
Weight: Rear axle	4,800 kg	10,582 lb.
Length (overall)	7,050 mm	23 ft., 1 ins.
Width (overall)	2,250 mm	7 ft., 4 ins.
Height (overall)	2,500 mm	8 ft., 2 ins.
Ground clearance	240 mm	9½ ins.
Tread centers	1,665 mm	5 ft., 5 ins.
	1,600 mm	5 ft., 3 ins.
Wheelbase	4,050 mm	159 ins.
Wheel width	190/400 mm	7½/15¾ ins.
Angle of approach		
Angle of departure		
Seating capacity		
Fording depth	550 mm	21 ins
Climbing ability		18°
Overturn gradient (lengthwise)		50°
Overturn gradient (crosswise)		40°
Turning radius	20 meters	65 ft., 7 ins.
Trailer load	3,000 kg	6,614 lb.
Engine horsepower	70 c–v	69 hp
Piston displacement	6,290 cu cm	377 cu. ins.
Fuel tank capacity	90 liters	23.8 gal.
Highway fuel consumption		6.7 m.p.g.
Average terrain fuel consumption..		

IRE ENGINE
S. 25 (o)

German nomenclature: Kraftfahrspritze (o) mit Fahrgestell des schwerer Lastkraftwagen (o).

English designation: Fire engine with special chassis of the heavy motor truck (standard commercial vehicle).

Net weight	7,800 kg	17,195 lb.
Pay load	650 kg	1,433 lb.
Gross weight	8,450 kg	18,628 lb.
Weight: Front axle	3,300 kg	7,275 lb.
Weight: Rear axle	5,150 kg	11,353 lb.
Length (overall)	8,685 mm	28 ft., 6 ins.
Width (overall)	2,200 mm	7 ft., 2 ins.
Height (overall)	2,700 mm	8 ft., 10 ins.
Ground clearance	100 mm	3⅞ ins.
Tread centers	1,700 mm	5 ft., 7 ins.
	2,000 mm	6 ft., 7 ins.
Wheelbase	4,575 mm	180 ins.
Wheel width	190–400 mm	7½/15¾ ins.
Angle of approach		20°
Angle of departure		10°
Seating capacity		9
Fording depth	180 mm	7 ins.
Climbing ability		17°
Overturn gradient (lengthwise)		50°
Overturn gradient (crosswise)		35°
Turning radius	17 meters	55 ft., 2 ins.
Trailer load		
Engine horsepower	125 c–v	123.3 hp
Piston displacement	9,122 cu cm	547 cu. ins.
Fuel tank capacity	120 liters	31.7 gal.
Highway fuel consumption		7.1 m.p.g.
Average terrain fuel consumption		

IRE FIGHTING WATER TANK
2, 5 (Kfz. 343)

German nomenclature: Tankspritze (Kfz. 343) mit Fahrgestell des mittleren geländegängiger Lastkraftwagen (o).

English designation: Fire fighting water tank with special chassis of the medium cross-country motor truck.

Net weight		
Pay load		
Gross weight	9,500 kg	20,943 lb.
Weight: Front axle	2,600 kg	5,732 lb.
Weight: Rear axle	3,450 kg	7,606 lb.
Length (overall)	7,880 mm	25 ft., 10 ins.
Width (overall)	2,220 mm	7 ft., 3 ins.
Height (overall)	2,280 mm	7 ft., 6 ins.
Ground clearance	270 mm	10⅝ ins.
Tread centers	1,850 mm	6 ft., 1 in.
	1,740 mm	5 ft., 8 ins.
	1,740 mm	5 ft., 8 ins.
Wheelbase	3,750/1,100 mm	148/43 ins.
Wheel width	190–400 mm	7½/15¾ ins.
Angle of approach		25°
Angle of departure		30°
Seating capacity		4
Fording depth	600 mm	23 ins.
Climbing ability		18°
Overturn gradient (lengthwise)		
Overturn gradient (crosswise)		34°
Turning radius		
Trailer load	4,000 kg	8,818 lb.
Engine horsepower	120 c–v	118.3 hp
Piston displacement	12,054 cu cm	723 cu. ins.
Fuel tank capacity	110 liters	29 gal.
Highway fuel consumption		7.1 m.p.g.
Average terrain fuel consumption		

HOSE TRUCK
S. W. (Kfz. 346)

German nomenclature: Schlauchkraftwagen (Kfz. 346) mit Fahrgestell des schwerer Lastkraftwagen (o).

English designation: Hose truck with special chassis of the heavy motor truck.

Net weight	9,641 kg	21,254 lb.
Pay load	600 kg	1,323 lb.
Gross weight	10,241 kg	22,577 lb.
Weight: Front axle	3,478 kg	7,667 lb.
Weight: Rear axle	6,763 kg	14,909 lb.
Length (overall)	7,983 mm	26 ft., 2 ins.
Width (overall)	2,200 mm	7 ft., 2 ins.
Height (overall)	2,750 mm	9 ft.
Ground clearance	185 mm	7¼ ins.
Tread centers	1,700 mm	5 ft., 7 ins.
	2,000 mm	6 ft., 7 ins.
Wheelbase	4,575 mm	180 ins.
Wheel width	208–500 mm	8⅛/20 ins.
Angle of approach		20°
Angle of departure		23°
Seating capacity		8
Fording depth	500 mm	20 ins.
Climbing ability		17°
Overturn gradient (lengthwise)		50°
Overturn gradient (crosswise)		35°
Turning radius	21 meters	68 ft., 11 ins.
Trailer load		
Engine horsepower	125 c–v	123.3 hp
Piston displacement	9,122 cu cm	547 cu. ins.
Fuel tank capacity	120 liters	31.7 gal.
Highway fuel consumption		7.1 m.p.g.
Average terrain fuel consumption		

HOSE TRUCK
St. (Kfz. 344)

German nomenclature: Schlauchtender (Kfz. 344) mit Fahrgestell des mittleren Lastkraftwagen (o).

English designation: Hose truck with special chassis of the medium motor truck.

Net weight	5,350 kg	11,795 lb.
Pay load	2,400 kg	5,292 lb.
Gross weight	7,750 kg	17,085 lb.
Weight: Front axle	2,580 kg	5,688 lb.
Weight: Rear axle	5,170 kg	11,397 lb.
Length (overall)	7,610 mm	25 ft.
Width (overall)	2,350 mm	7 ft., 8 ins.
Height (overall)	2,250 mm	7 ft., 4 ins.
Ground clearance	235 mm	9¼ ins.
Tread centers	1,700 mm	5 ft., 7 ins.
	2,000 mm	6 ft., 7 ins.
Wheelbase	4,600 mm	181 ins.
Wheel width	190–400 mm	7½/15¾ ins.
Angle of approach		30°
Angle of departure		20°
Seating capacity		7
Fording depth	700 mm	27 ins.
Climbing ability		18°
Overturn gradient (lengthwise)		60°
Overturn gradient (crosswise)		40°
Turning radius	25 meters	82 ft.
Trailer load		
Engine horsepower	100 c–v	98.6 hp
Piston displacement	7,413 cu cm	445 cu. ins.
Fuel tank capacity	130 liters	34.3 gal.
Highway fuel consumption		5.2–7.8 m.p.g.
Average terrain fuel consumption		

MOTORIZED FIRE FIGHTING LADDER
L. 26 (o)

German nomenclature: Kraftfahrdrehleiter 26 meters (o) mit Fahrgestell des schwerer Lastkraftwagen (o).

English designation: Motorized fire fighting ladder (26 meters (85 ft., 4 ins.) with special chassis of the heavy motor truck (standard commercial vehicle).

Net weight	9,400 kg	20,723 lb.
Pay load	500 kg	1,102 lb.
Gross weight	9,900 kg	21,825 lb.
Weight: Front axle	3,900 kg	8,597 lb.
Weight: Rear axle	6,000 kg	13,227 lb.
Length (overall)	7,700 mm	28 ft., 6 ins.
Width (overall)	2,200 mm	7 ft., 2 ins.
Height (overall)	2,750 mm	9 ft.
Ground clearance	200 mm	8¼ ins.
Tread centers	1,700 mm	5 ft., 7 ins.
	2,000 mm	6 ft., 7 ins.
Wheelbase	4,800 mm	189 ins.
Wheel width	190–400 mm	7½/15¾ ins.
Angle of approach		20°
Angle of departure		14°
Seating capacity		6
Fording depth	500 mm	20 ins.
Climbing ability		18°
Overturn gradient (lengthwise)		50°
Overturn gradient (crosswise)		35°
Turning radius	17 meters	55 ft., 2 ins.
Trailer load		
Engine horsepower	125 c–v	123.3 hp
Piston displacement	9,400 cu cm	564 cu. ins.
Fuel tank capacity	120 liters	31.7 gal.
Highway fuel consumption		7.1 m.p.g.
Average terrain fuel consumption		

OXYGEN TANK TRUCK
Sauerstoff-Kessel-Kw. (Kfz. 317)

German nomenclature: Sauerstoff-Kesselkraftwagen (Kfz. 317) (schwerer Lastkraftwagen (o)).

English designation: Oxygen tank truck (heavy motor truck).

Net weight	8,000 kg	17,637 lb.
Pay load	5,000 kg	11,023 lb.
Gross weight	13,000 kg	28,660 lb.
Weight: Front axle	5,000 kg	11,023 lb.
Weight: Rear axle	8,000 kg	17,636 lb.
Length (overall)	8,100 mm	
Width (overall)	3,120 mm	
Height (overall)	3,120 mm	10 ft., 3 ins.
Ground clearance	200 mm	7⅞ ins.
Tread centers	2,000 mm	6 ft., 7 ins.
	2,200 mm	7 ft., 2 ins.
Wheelbase	5,100 mm	200 ins.
Wheel width	190 (front)–	7½ ins. (front)
	400 (rear)	15¾ ins. (rear)
Angle of approach		45°
Angle of departure		30°
Seating capacity		
Fording depth	550 mm	21 ins.
Climbing ability		30°
Overturn gradient (lengthwise)		50°
Overturn gradient (crosswise)		30°
Turning radius	20 meters	65 ft., 7 ins.
Trailer load	8,000 kg	17,636 lb.
Engine horsepower	150 c–v	147.9 hp
Piston displacement	12,517 cu cm	751 cu. ins.
Fuel tank capacity	150 liters	39.6 gal.
Highway fuel consumption		5.9–7.8 m.p.g.
Average terrain fuel consumption		

LIGHT TRACTOR
l. Rd. Schlp. (o)

German nomenclature: leichter Radschlepper (o).

English designation: Light tractor (standard commercial vehicle).

Net weight	2,000 kg	4,409 lb.
Pay load		
Gross weight	2,000 kg	4,409 lb.
Weight: Front axle	700 kg	1,543 lb.
Weight: Rear axle	1,300 kg	2,866 lb.
Length (overall)	3,400 mm	11 ft., 2 ins.
Width (overall)	1,800 mm	5 ft., 11 ins.
Height (overall)	1,700 mm	5 ft., 7 ins.
Ground clearance	200 mm	7⅞ ins.
Tread centers	1,300 mm	4 ft., 3 ins.
	1,450 mm	4 ft., 9 ins.
Wheelbase	2,220 mm	87 ins.
Wheel width	230 mm	9 ins.
Angle of approach		90°
Angle of departure		50°
Seating capacity		1
Fording depth	450 mm	18 ins.
Climbing ability		
Overturn gradient (lengthwise)		
Overturn gradient (crosswise)		35°
Turning radius	9 meters	29 ft., 6 ins.
Engine horsepower	25 c—v	24.7 hp
Piston displacement	3,500 cu cm	210 cu. ins.
Fuel tank capacity	120 liters	31.7 gal.
Highway fuel consumption		5.9—7.8 m.p.g.
Average terrain fuel consumption		

MEDIUM TRACTOR
m. Rd. Schlp. (o)

German nomenclature: mittlerer Radschlepper (o).

English designation: Medium tractor (standard commercial vehicle).

Net weight	3,800 kg	8,377 lb.
Weight: Front axle	900 kg	1,984 lb.
Weight: Rear axle	2,900 kg	6,393 lb.
Length (overall)	3,500 mm	11 ft., 6 ins.
Width (overall)	2,000 mm	6 ft., 7 ins.
Height (overall)	2,200 mm	7 ft., 2 ins.
Ground clearance	250 mm	9⅞ ins.
Tread centers	1,500 mm	4 ft., 11 ins.
	1,600 mm	5 ft., 3 ins.
Wheelbase	2,200 mm	86 ins.
Wheel width	260 mm	10¼ ins.
Angle of approach		90°
Angle of departure		60°
Seating capacity		1
Fording depth	500 mm	20 ins.
Climbing ability		
Overturn gradient (lengthwise)		45°
Overturn gradient (crosswise)		40°
Turning radius	11 meters	36 ft., 1 in.
Engine horsepower	45 c—v	44.4 hp
Piston displacement	6,000 cu cm	360 cu. ins.
Fuel tank capacity	150 liters	39.6 gal.
Highway fuel consumption		4.7—6.7 m.p.g.
Average terrain fuel consumption		

HEAVY TRACTOR
Rd. Schlp. (o)

German nomenclature: schwerer Radschlepper (o).

English designation: Heavy tractor (standard commercial vehicle).

Net weight	6,450 kg	23,147 lb.
Pay load		
Gross weight		
Weight: Front axle	2,370 kg	7,209 lb.
Weight: Rear axle	4,170 kg	9,193 lb.
Length (overall)	5,545 mm	18 ft. 2 ins.
Width (overall)	2,460 mm	8 ft.
Height (overall)	2,420 mm	7 ft., 11 ins.
Ground clearance	270 mm	10⅝ ins.
Tread centers	1,908 mm	6 ft., 2 ins.
	1,836 mm	6 ft.
Wheelbase	3,000 mm	118 ins.
Wheel width	300 mm	11⅞ ins.
Angle of approach		40°
Angle of departure		17°
Seating capacity		5
Fording depth		
Climbing ability		5°
Overturn gradient (lengthwise)		50°
Overturn gradient (crosswise)		35°
Turning radius	10.5 meters	34 ft., 5 ins.
Trailer load	15,000 kg	33,069 lb.
Engine horsepower	100 c–v	98.6 hp
Piston displacement	8,553 cu cm	513 cu. ins.
Fuel tank capacity	350 liters	92.4 gal.
Highway fuel consumption		5.2 m.p.g.
Average terrain fuel consumption		3.9 m.p.g.

LIGHT TRACTOR
Kett. Schlp. (o)

German nomenclature: leichter Kettenschlepper (o).

English designation: Light tractor (standard commercial vehicle).

Net weight	3,500 kg	7,716 lb.
Pay load		
Gross weight		
Weight: Front axle		
Weight: Rear axle		
Length (overall)	3,100 mm	10 ft., 2 ins.
Width (overall)	1,550 mm	5 ft., 1 in.
Height (overall)	2,300 mm	7 ft., 6 ins.
Ground clearance	310 mm	12⅛ ins.
Tread centers	1,300 mm	4 ft., 3 ins.
Track contact	0.85 mm	33½ ins.
Track width	300 mm	11⅞ ins.
Angle of approach		40°
Angle of departure		65°
Seating capacity		
Fording depth	700 mm	27 ins.
Climbing ability		30°
Overturn gradient (lengthwise)		45°
Overturn gradient (crosswise)		40°
Turning radius	7 meters	22 ft., 11 ins.
Trailer load	5,000 kg	11,023 lb.
Lifting power of winch	3,000 kg	6,614 lb.
Engine horsepower	45 c–v	44.4 hp
Piston displacement	5,500 cu cm	330 cu. ins.
Fuel tank capacity	65 liters	17.2 gal.
Highway fuel consumption		6.7 m.p.g.
Average terrain fuel consumption		4.7 m.p.g.

MEDIUM TRACTOR
m. Kett. Schlp. (o)

German nomenclature: mittlerer Kettenschlepper (o).

English designation: Medium tractor (standard commercial vehicle).

Net weight	4,600 kg	10,194 lb.
Length (overall)	3,300 mm	10 ft., 10 ins.
Width (overall)	1,550 mm	5 ft., 1 in.
Height (overall)	1,450 mm	4 ft., 9 ins.
Ground clearance	270 mm	10 ft., 10 ins.
Tread centers	1,300 mm	4 ft., 3 ins.
Track contact	1.1 mm	43 ins.
Track width	300 mm	11⅞ ins.
Angle of approach		40°
Angle of departure		70°
Seating capacity		
Fording depth	600 mm	23 ins.
Climbing ability		35°
Overturn gradient (lengthwise)		45°
Overturn gradient (crosswise)		40°
Turning radius	7 meters	22 ft., 11 ins.
Trailer load	6,000 kg	13,227 lb.
Lifting power of winch	3,000 kg	6,614 lb.
Engine horsepower	65 c—v	64.1 hp
Piston displacement	9,000 cu cm	540 cu. ins.
Fuel tank capacity	90 liters	23.8 gal.
Highway fuel consumption		3.9 m.p.g.
Average terrain fuel consumption		

LIGHT FULL-TRACKED PRIME MOVER
l. R.-Schlepper (Praga T 3)

German nomenclature: leichter Raupenschlepper (Praga T 3).

English designation: Light full-tracked prime mover.

Net weight	4,650 kg	10,249 lb.
Pay load	550 kg	1,652 lb.
Gross weight	5,400 kg	11,902 lb.
Length (overall)	4,100 mm	13 ft., 5 ins.
Width (overall)	1,730 mm	5 ft., 8 ins.
Height (overall)	2,300 mm	7 ft., 6 ins.
Ground clearance	400 mm	15¾ ins.
Tread centers	1,420 mm	4 ft., 8 ins.
Track contact	2 mm	79 ins.
Track width	300 mm	11⅞ ins.
Angle of approach		
Angle of departure		
Seating capacity		3
Fording depth	550 mm	21⅝ ins.
Climbing ability		30°
Overturn gradient (lengthwise)		40°
Overturn gradient (crosswise)		30°
Turning radius	3 meters	118 ins.
Trailer load	1,800 kg	3,967 lb.
Lifting power of winch	3,000 kg	6,612 lb.
Engine horsepower	70 c—v	65 hp
Piston displacement	4,300 cu cm	258 cu. ins.
Fuel tank capacity	150 liters	39.6 gal.
Highway fuel consumption		2.93 m.p.g.
Average terrain fuel consumption		2.14 m.p.g.

HEAVY FULL-TRACKED PRIME MOVER

s. R.-Schlepper (Praga T 9)

German nomenclature: schwerer Raupenschlepper (Praga T 9).

English designation: Heavy full-tracked prime mover.

Net weight	10,100 kg	22,260 lb.
Gross weight	11,600 kg	25,566 lb.
Length (overall)	5,600 mm	18 ft., 4 ins.
Width (overall)	2,450 mm	8 ft.
Height (overall)	2,540 mm	8 ft., 4 ins.
Ground clearance	340 mm	13 ins.
Tread centers	2,070 mm	6 ft., 9 ins.
Track contact	3.2 mm	126 ins.
Track width	340 mm	13¼ ins.
Ti ɔ size		
Angle of approach		
Angle of departure		
Seating capacity		8
Fording depth	700 mm	27¼ ins.
Climbing ability		50°
Overturn gradient (lengthwise)		45°
Overturn gradient (crosswise)		35°
Turning radius	3 meters	9 ft., 10 ins.
Trailer load	15,000 kg	33,060 lb.
Lifting power of winch	7,500 kg	16,530 lb.
Engine horsepower	140 c-v	130 hp
Piston displacement	14,230 cu cm	854 cu. ins.
Fuel tank capacity	250 liters	66 gal.
Highway fuel consumption		1.49 m.p.g.
Average terrain fuel consumption		1.18 m.p.g.

MACHINE GUN CAR

M. G. Kw. (Kfz. 13)

German nomenclature: Maschinengewehrkraftwagen (Kfz. 13) mit Fahrgestell des mittleren Panzerkraftwagen (o).

English designation: Machine gun car with special chassis for the medium armored car.

Net weight	1,900 kg	4,188 lb.
Gross weight	2,200 kg	4,850 lb.
Weight: Front axle	900 kg	1,984 lb.
Weight: Rear axle	1,300 kg	2,866 lb.
Length (overall)	4,200 mm	13 ft., 9 ins.
Width (overall)	1,700 mm	5 ft., 7 ins.
Height (overall)	1,500 mm	4 ft., 11 ins.
Ground clearance	180 mm	7⅛ ins.
Tread centers	1,430 mm	4 ft., 8 ins.
Wheelbase	2,840 mm	112 ins.
Wheel width	170 mm	6¾ ins.
Angle of approach		55°
Angle of departure		35°
Seating capacity		
Fording depth	500 mm	20 ins.
Climbing ability		15°
Overturn gradient (lengthwise)		50°
Overturn gradient (crosswise)		30°
Turning radius	15 meters	49 ft., 2 ins.
Trailer load		
Engine horsepower	60 c-v	59.2 hp
Piston displacement	3,000 cu cm	180 cu. ins.
Fuel tank capacity	70 liters	18.5 gal.
Highway fuel consumption		9.4 m.p.g.
Average terrain fuel consumption		6.7 m.p.g.

RADIO CAR
Fu. Kw. (Kfz. 14)

Net weight	1,900 kg	4,188 lb.
Pay load	350 kg	772 lb.
Gross weight	2,250 kg	4,960 lb.
Weight: Front axle	900 kg	1,984 lb.
Weight: Rear axle	1,350 kg	2,975 lb.
Length (overall)	4,200 mm	13 ft., 9 ins.
Width (overall)	1,700 mm	5 ft., 7 ins.
Height (overall)	1,500 mm	4 ft., 11 ins.
Ground clearance	180 mm	7⅛ ins.
Tread centers	1,430 mm	4 ft., 8 ins.
Wheelbase	2,840 mm	112 ins.
Wheel width	170 mm	6¾ ins.
Angle of approach		55°
Angle of departure		35°
Seating capacity		
Fording depth	500 mm	20 ins.
Climbing ability		15°
Overturn gradient (lengthwise)		50°
Overturn gradient (crosswise)		30°
Turning radius	15 meters	49 ft., 2 ins.
Trailer load		
Engine horsepower	60 c—v	59.2 hp
Piston displacement	3,000 cu cm	180 cu. ins.
Fuel tank capacity	70 liters	18.5 gal.
Highway fuel consumption		9.4 m.p.g.
Average terrain fuel consumption		6.7 m.p.g.

German nomenclature: Funkkraftwagen (Kfz. 14) mit Fahrgestell des mittleren Panzerkraftwagen (o).

English designation: Radio car with special chassis of the medium armored car.

HEAVY CROSS-COUNTRY ARMORED PERSONNEL CAR
s. gl. gp. Pkw. (Sd. Kfz. 247)

Net weight	4,600 kg	10,194 lb.
Pay load	600 kg	1,269 lb.
Gross weight	5,200 kg	11,463 lb.
Weight: Front axle	1,400 kg	3,086 lb.
Weight: Rear axle	1,900 kg	4,188 lb.
Length (overall)	4,600 mm	15 ft., 1 in.
Width (overall)	1,960 mm	6 ft., 5 ins.
Height (overall)	1,700 mm	5 ft., 7 ins.
Ground clearance	240 mm	9½ ins.
Tread centers	1,580 mm	5 ft., 2 ins.
	1,565 mm	5 ft., 1 in.
	1,565 mm	5 ft., 1 in.
Wheelbase	2,445/900 mm	96/35 ins.
Wheel width	190 mm	7½ ins.
Angle of approach		50°
Angle of departure		40°
Seating capacity		6
Fording depth	600 mm	23 ins.
Climbing ability		20°
Overturn gradient (lengthwise)		50°
Overturn gradient (crosswise)		35°
Turning radius	16 meters	52 ft., 6 ins.
Trailer load	1,000 kg	2,205 lb.
Engine horsepower	65 c—v	64.1 hp
Piston displacement	3,500 cu cm	210 cu. ins.
Fuel tank capacity	110 liters	29 gal.
Highway fuel consumption		7.8 m.p.g.
Average terrain fuel consumption		4.7 m.p.g.

German nomenclature: schwerer geländegängig gepanzerte Personenkraftwagen (Sd. Kfz. 247) mit Fahrgestell des leichter geländegängiger Lastkraftwagen (o).

English designation: Heavy cross-country armored personnel car with special chassis of the light cross-country truck.

HEAVY CROSS-COUNTRY ARMORED PERSONNEL CAR
s. gl. gp. Pkw. (Sd. Kfz. 247)

German nomenclature: schwerer geländegängig gepanzerte Personenkraftwagen (Sd. Kfz. 247) mit Einheitsfahrgestell II für schwerer Panzerkraftwagen.

English designation: Heavy cross-country armored personnel car with standard chassis II for heavy armored car.

Net weight	3,700 kg	8,157 lb.
Pay load	760 kg	1,675 lb.
Gross weight	4,460 kg	9,832 lb.
Weight: Front axle	2,260 kg	4,982 lb.
Weight: Rear axle	2,200 kg	4,850 lb.
Length (overall)	5,000 mm	16 ft., 5 ins.
Width (overall)	2,000 mm	6 ft., 7 ins.
Height (overall)	1,800 mm	5 ft., 11 ins.
Ground clearance	230 mm	9 ins.
Tread centers	1,640 mm	5 ft., 4 ins.
	1,640 mm	5 ft., 4 ins.
Wheelbase	3,000 mm	118 ins.
Wheel width		
Angle of approach		50°
Angle of departure		35°
Seating capacity		6
Fording depth	500 mm	20 ins.
Climbing ability		21°
Overturn gradient (lengthwise)		40°
Overturn gradient (crosswise)		35°
Turning radius	13.50/9 meters	44 ft., 3 ins./29 ft., 6 ins.
Trailer load		
Engine horsepower	75 c–v	74 hp
Piston displacement	3,500 cu cm	210 cu. ins.
Fuel tank capacity	160 liters	42.2 gal.
Highway fuel consumption		6.7 m.p.g.
Average terrain fuel consumption		4.3 m.p.g.

LIGHT ARMORED SCOUT CAR
Pz. Sp. Wg. (Sd. Kfz. 221)

German nomenclature: leichter Panzerspähwagen (Sd. Kfz. 221) mit Einheitsfahrgestell I für schwerer Panzerkraftwagen.

English designation: Light armored scout car with standard chassis I for heavy armored car.

Net weight	3,750 kg	8,267 lb.
Pay load		
Gross weight	4,000 kg	8,818 lb.
Weight: Front axle	1,500 kg	3,307 lb.
Weight: Rear axle	2,500 kg	5,512 lb.
Length (overall)	4,800 mm	15 ft., 9 ins.
Width (overall)	1,950 mm	6 ft., 5 ins.
Height (overall)	1,700 mm	5 ft., 7 ins.
Ground clearance		
Tread centers	1,610 mm	5 ft., 3 ins.
Wheelbase	2,800 mm	110 ins.
Wheel width	190 mm	7½ ins.
Angle of approach		50°
Angle of departure		35°
Seating capacity		
Fording depth	600 mm	23 ins.
Climbing ability		22°
Overturn gradient (lengthwise)		40°
Overturn gradient (crosswise)		30°
Turning radius	15/8 meters	49 ft., 2 ins./26 ft., 3 ins.
Trailer load		
Engine horsepower		
Piston displacement		
Fuel tank capacity	110 liters	29 gal.
Highway fuel consumption		7.1 m.p.g.
Average terrain fuel consumption		4.3 m.p.g.

LIGHT ARMORED SCOUT CAR
l. Pz. Sp. Wg. (Sd. Kfz. 222)

German nomenclature: leichter Panzerspähwagen (Sd. Kfz. 222) mit Einheitsfahrgestell I für schwerer Panzerkraftwagen.

English designation: Light armored scout car with standard chassis I for heavy armored car.

Net weight	3,750 kg	8,267 lb.
Pay load	1,050 kg	2,315 lb.
Gross weight	4,800 kg	10,582 lb.
Weight: Front axle	1,850 kg	4,078 lb.
Weight: Rear axle	2,950 kg	6,503 lb.
Length (overall)	4,800 mm	15 ft., 9 ins.
Width (overall)	1,950 mm	6 ft., 5 ins.
Height (overall)	2,000 mm	6 ft., 7 ins.
Ground clearance	230 mm	9 ins.
Tread centers	1,610 mm	5 ft., 3 ins.
Wheelbase	2,800 mm	110 ins.
Wheel width	190 mm	7½ ins.
Angle of approach		50°
Angle of departure		35°
Seating capacity		
Fording depth	600 mm	23 ins.
Climbing ability		20°
Overturn gradient (lengthwise)		40°
Overturn gradient (crosswise)		30°
Turning radius	14 meters (front wheels)	46 ft., 4 ins.
	8 meters (all wheels)	26 ft., 3 ins.
Engine horsepower	75 c-v	74 hp
Piston displacement	3,500 cu cm	210 cu. ins.
Fuel tank capacity	110 liters	29 gal.
Highway fuel consumption		6.5 m.p.g.
Average terrain fuel consumption		4 m.p.g.

LIGHT ARMORED SCOUT CAR
l. Pz. Sp. Wg. (Fu.) (Sd. Kfz. 223)

German nomenclature: leichter Panzerspähwagen (Fu.) (Sd. Kfz. 223) mit Einheitsfahrgestell I für schwerer Panzerkraftwagen.

English designation: Light armored scout car with standard chassis I for heavy armored car.

Net weight	3,950 kg	8,707 lb.
Pay load	450 kg	193 lb.
Gross weight	4,400 kg	9,700 lb.
Weight: Front axle	1,650 kg	3,637 lb.
Weight: Rear axle	2,750 kg	6,062 lb.
Length (overall)	4,800 mm	15 ft., 9 ins.
Width (overall)	1,950 mm	6 ft., 5 ins.
Height (overall)	1,750 mm	5 ft., 9 ins.
Ground clearance	230 mm	9 ins.
Tread centers	1,610 mm	5 ft., 3 ins.
Wheelbase	2,800 mm	110 ins.
Wheel width	190 mm	7½ ins.
Angle of approach		50°
Angle of departure		35°
Seating capacity		
Fording depth	600 mm	23 ins.
Climbing ability		20°
Overturn gradient (lengthwise)		40°
Overturn gradient (crosswise)		30°
Turning radius	14 meters (front wheel)	46 ft., 4 ins.
	8 meters (all wheels)	26 ft., 3 ins.
Trailer load		
Engine horsepower	75 c-v	74 hp
Piston displacement	3,500 cu cm	210 cu. ins.
Fuel tank capacity	110 liters	29 gal.
Highway fuel consumption		6.7 m.p.g.
Average terrain fuel consumption		4.3 m.p.g.

HEAVY ARMORED SCOUT CAR
s. Pz. Sp. Wg. (Sd. Kfz. 231)

Net weight	5,300 kg	11,684 lb.
Pay load	700 kg	1,543 lb.
Gross weight	6,000 kg	13,227 lb.
Weight: Front axle	1,850 kg	4,078 lb.
Weight: Rear axle	2,075 kg	4,574 lb.
Length (overall)	5,600 mm	18 ft., 4 ins.
Width (overall)	1,850 mm	6 ft., 1 in.
Height (overall)	2,250 mm	7 ft., 4 ins.
Ground clearance	200 mm	8 ins.
Tread centers	1,840 mm	6 ft.
Wheelbase	2,500/900 mm	98/35 ins.
Wheel width		
Angle of approach		55°
Angle of departure		40°
Seating capacity		
Fording depth	600 mm	23 ins.
Climbing ability		13°
Overturn gradient (lengthwise)		55°
Overturn gradient (crosswise)		35°
Turning radius	16 meters	52 ft., 6 ins.
Trailer load		
Engine horsepower	70 c–v	69 hp
Piston displacement	4,600 cu cm	276 cu. ins.
Fuel tank capacity	100 liters	26.4 gal.
Highway fuel consumption		5.9 m.p.g.
Average terrain fuel consumption		3.6 m.p.g.

German nomenclature: schwerer Panzerspähwagen (Sd. Kfz. 231) mit Fahrgestell des leichter geländegängiger Lastkraftwagen (o).

English designation: Heavy armored scout car with special chassis of the light cross-country truck (standard commercial vehicle).

HEAVY ARMORED SCOUT CAR (8 WHEELS)
s. Pz. Sp. Wg. (Sd. Kfz. 231) (8 Rad)

Net weight	7,600 kg	16,720 lb.
Pay load	700 kg	1,578 lb.
Gross weight	8,300 kg	18,298 lb.
Weight: Front axle	2,050 kg	4,519 lb.
Weight: Rear axle	2,100 kg	4,630 lb.
Length (overall)	5,850 mm	19 ft., 2 ins.
Width (overall)	2,200 mm	7 ft., 2 ins.
Height (overall)	2,350 mm	7 ft., 8 ins.
Ground clearance	270 mm	10½ ins.
Tread centers	1,600 mm	5 ft., 3 ins.
Wheelbase	1,350/1,400/ 1,350 mm	53/55/53 ins.
Wheel width	190 mm	7½ ins.
Angle of approach		60°
Angle of departure		60°
Seating capacity		
Fording depth	1,000 mm	39 ins.
Climbing ability		30°
Overturn gradient (lengthwise)		
Overturn gradient (crosswise)		35°
Turning radius	10.5 meters (all wheels)	34 ft., 5 ins.
Trailer load		
Engine horsepower	160 c–v	157.8 hp
Piston displacement	7,600 cu cm	456 cu. ins.
Fuel tank capacity	180 liters	47.5 gal.
Highway fuel consumption		3.9 m.p.g.
Average terrain fuel consumption		2.2 m.p.g.

German nomenclature: schwerer Panzerspähwagen (Sd. Kfz. 231) (8 Rad).

English designation: Heavy armored scout car (8 wheels).

HEAVY ARMORED SCOUT CAR
s. Pz. Sp. Wg. (Fu.) (Sd. Kfz. 232)

German nomenclature: schwerer Panzerspähwagen (Fu.) (Sd. Kfz. 232) mit Fahrgestell des leichter geländegängiger Lastkraftwagen (o).

English designation: Heavy armored scout car with special chassis of the light cross-country truck.

Net weight	5,500 kg	12,125 lb.
Pay load		
Gross weight	6,250 kg	13,778 lb.
Weight: Front axle	1,900 kg	4,188 lb.
Weight Rear axle	2,175 kg	4,795 lb.
Length (overall)	5,600 mm	18 ft., 4 ins.
Height (overall)	2,900 mm	9 ft., 6 ins.
Ground clearance	240 mm	9½ ins.
Tread centers	1,700 mm	5 ft., 7 ins.
	1,840 mm	6 ft.
Wheelbase	2,500/900 mm	98/35 ins.
Wheel width	170/350 mm	6¾/13¾ ins.
Angle of approach		55°
Angle of departure		40°
Seating capacity		
Fording depth	600 mm	23 ins.
Climbing ability		13°
Overturn gradient (lengthwise)		55°
Overturn gradient (crosswise)		35°
Turning radius	16 meters	52 ft., 6 ins.
Trailer load		
Engine horsepower	70 c–v	69 hp
Piston displacement	4,600 cu cm	276 cu. ins.
Fuel tank capacity	100 liters	26.4 gal.
Highway fuel consumption		5.9 m.p.g.
Average terrain fuel consumption		3.6 m.p.g.

HEAVY ARMORED SCOUT CAR (8 WHEELS)
s. Pz. Sp. Wg. (Fu.) (Sd. Kfz. 232) (8 Rad)

German nomenclature: schwerer Panzerspähwagen (Fu.) (Sd. Kfz. 232) (8 Rad).

English designation: Heavy armored scout car (8 wheels).

Net weight	7,700 kg	16,975 lb.
Pay load		
Gross weight	8,500 kg	18,739 lb.
Weight: Front axle	2,100 kg	4,630 lb.
Weight: Rear axle	2,500 kg	5,512 lb.
Length (overall)	5,850 mm	19 ft., 2 ins.
Width (overall)	2,200 mm	7 ft., 3 ins.
Height (overall)	2,900 mm	9 ft., 6 ins.
Ground clearance	500 mm	20 ins.
Tread centers	1,600 mm	5 ft., 3 ins.
Wheelbase	1,350/1,400/ 1,350 mm	53/55/53 ins.
Wheel width	190 mm	7½ ins.
Angle of approach		60°
Angle of departure		60°
Seating capacity		
Fording depth	1,000 mm	39 ins.
Climbing ability		30°
Overturn gradient (lengthwise)		
Overturn gradient (crosswise)		35°
Turning radius	10.5 meters (all wheels)	34 ft., 5 ins.
Trailer load		
Engine horsepower	160 c–v	157.8 hp
Piston displacement	8,000 cu cm	480 cu. ins.
Fuel tank capacity	180 liters	47.5 gal.
Highway fuel consumption		3.9 m.p.g.
Average terrain fuel consumption		2.2 m.p.g.

SMALL ARMORED RADIO CAR
:l. Pz. Fu. Wg. (Sd. Kfz. 260)

erman nomenclature: kleiner Panzerfunkwagen (Sd. Kfz. 260) mit Einheitsfahrgestell I für schwerer Panzerkraftwagen.

nglish designation: Small armored radio car with standard chassis I for heavy armored car.

Net weight	3,815 kg	8,416 lb.
Pay load		
Gross weight	4,260 kg	9,390 lb.
Weight: Front axle	1,565 kg	3,450 lb.
Weight: Rear axle	2,695 kg	5,941 lb.
Length (overall)	4,830 mm	15 ft., 10 ins.
Width (overall)	1,990 mm	6 ft. 6 ins.
Height (overall)	1,780 mm	5 ft., 10 ins.
Ground clearance	240 mm	9½ ins.
Tread centers	1,610 mm	5 ft., 3 ins.
Wheelbase	2,800 mm	110 ins.
Wheel width	190 mm	7½ ins.
Angle of approach		50°
Angle of departure		35°
Seating capacity		
Fording depth	600 mm	23 ins.
Climbing ability		22°
Overturn gradient (lengthwise)		40°
Overturn gradient (crosswise)		30°
Turning radius		
Trailer load		
Engine horsepower	75 c–v	74 hp
Piston displacement	3,500 cu cm	210 cu. ins.
Fuel tank capacity	110 liters	29 gal.
Highway fuel consumption		6.7 m.p.g.
Average terrain fuel consumption		4.3 m.p.g.

SMALL ARMORED RADIO CAR
. Pz. Fu. Wg. (Sd. Kfz. 261)

erman nomenclature: kleiner Panzerfunkwagen (Sd. Kfz. 261) mit Einheitsfahrgestell I für schwerer Panzerkraftwagen.

glish designation: Small armored radio car with standard chassis I for heavy armored car.

Net weight	3,855 kg	8,498 lb.
Pay load		
Gross weight	4,300 kg	9,480 lb.
Weight: Front axle	1,585 kg	3,494 lb.
Weight: Rear axle	2,715 kg	5,985 lb.
Length (overall)	4,830 mm	15 ft., 10 ins.
Width (overall)	1,990 mm	6 ft. 6 ins.
Height (overall)	1,780 mm	5 ft., 10 ins.
Ground clearance	240 mm	9½ ins.
Tread centers	1,610 mm	5 ft., 3 ins.
Wheelbase	2,800 mm	110 ins.
Wheel width	190 mm	7½ ins.
Angle of approach		50°
Angle of departure		35°
Seating capacity		
Fording depth	600 mm	23 ins.
Climbing ability		22°
Overturn gradient (lengthwise)		40°
Overturn gradient (crosswise)		30°
Turning radius		
Trailer load		
Engine horsepower	75 c–v	74 hp
Piston displacement	3,500 cu cm	210 cu. ins.
Fuel tank capacity	110 liters	29 gal.
Highway fuel consumption		6.7 m.p.g.
Average terrain fuel consumption		4.3 m.p.g.

ARMORED RADIO CAR
Pz. Fu. Wg. (Sd. Kfz. 263)

German nomenclature: Panzerfunkwagen (Sd. Kfz. 263) mit Fahrgestell des leichter geländegängiger Lastkraftwagen (o).

English designation: Armored radio car with special chassis of the light cross-country truck.

Net weight	5,250 kg	11,573 lb.
Pay load		
Gross weight	5,800 kg	12,786 lb.
Weight: Front axle	1,800 kg	3,968 lb.
Weight: Rear axle	2,000 kg	4,409 lb.
Length (overall)	5,570 mm	18 ft., 4 ins.
Height (overall)	2,930 mm	9 ft., 7 ins.
Ground clearance	240 mm	9½ ins.
Tread centers	1,700 mm	5 ft., 7 ins.
	1,840 mm	6 ft.
Wheelbase	2,500/900 mm	98/35 ins.
Wheel width	170—350 mm	6¾/13¾ ins.
Tire size		
Angle of approach		55°
Angle of departure		40°
Seating capacity		
Fording depth	600 mm	23 ins.
Climbing ability		13°
Overturn gradient (lengthwise)		55°
Overturn gradient (crosswise)		35°
Turning radius	16 meters	52 ft., 6 ins.
Trailer load		
Lifting power of winch		
Engine horsepower	70 c—v	69 hp
Piston displacement	4,600 cu cm	276 cu. ins.
Fuel tank capacity	100 liters	26.4 gal.
Highway fuel consumption		5.9 m.p.g.
Average terrain fuel consumption		3.6 m.p.g.

ARMORED RADIO CAR
Pz. Fu. Wg. (Sd. Kfz. 263) (8 Rad)

German nomenclature: Panzerfunkwagen (Sd. Kfz. 263) (8 Rad).

English designation: Armored radio car (8 wheels).

Net weight	7,550 kg	16,644 lb.
Pay load		
Gross weight	8,100 kg	17,857 lb.
Weight: Front axle	1,950 kg	4,298 lb.
Weight: Rear axle	2,100 kg	4,630 lb.
Length (overall)	5,850 mm	19 ft., 2 ins.
Width (overall)	2,200 mm	7 ft., 3 ins.
Height (overall)	2,900 mm	9 ft., 6 ins.
Ground clearance	270 mm	10½ ins.
Tread centers	1,600 mm	5 ft., 3 ins.
Wheelbase	1,350/1,400/ 1,350 mm	53/55/53 ins.
Wheel width	190 mm	7½ ins.
Tire size		
Angle of approach		60°
Angle of departure		60°
Seating capacity		
Fording depth	1,000 mm	39 ins.
Climbing ability		30°
Overturn gradient (lengthwise)		
Overturn gradient (crosswise)		35°
Turning radius	10.5 meters (all wheels)	34 ft., 5 ins.
Trailer load		
Lifting power of winch		
Engine horsepower	160 c—v	157.8 hp
Piston displacement	8,000 cu cm	480 cu. ins.
Fuel tank capacity	180 liters	47.5 gal.
Highway fuel consumption		3.9 m.p.g.
Average terrain fuel consumption		2.2 m.p.g.

SIDE CAR FOR MOTORCYCLE

Beiwg. für Krad. (o)

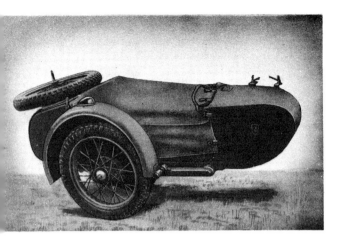

Net weight	110 kg	242 lb.
Pay load	220 kg	485 lb.
Gross weight	330 kg	727 lb.
Length (overall)	1,950 mm	6 ft., 5 ins.
Width (overall)	1,020 mm	3 ft., 4 ins.
Height (overall)	750 mm	2 ft., 6 ins.
Ground clearance	160 mm	6¼ ins.
Tread centers		
Wheel width	130 mm	5⅛ ins.
Angle of approach		
Angle of departure		24°
Seating capacity		1
Fording depth		

German nomenclature: Beiwagen für Kraftrad (o) (Einheitsbeiwagen).

English designation: Side car for motorcycle (standard commercial vehicle).

TRAILER (OPEN)

Anh. (1 achs.) off. (o)

Net weight	500 kg	1,102 lb.
Pay load	300 kg	660 lb.
Gross weight	800 kg	1,764 lb.
Weight: axle	800 kg	1,764 lb.
Length (overall)	2,100 mm	6 ft., 11 ins.
Width (overall)	1,500 mm	4 ft., 11 ins.
Height (overall)	1,100 mm	3 ft., 7 ins.
Ground clearance	200 mm	7⅞ ins.
Tread centers	1,300 mm	4 ft., 3 ins.
Wheel width	120 mm	4¾ ins.
Angle of approach		
Angle of departure		
Fording depth		
Overturn gradient (crosswise)		45°

German nomenclature: Anhänger (1 achs.) offen (o).

English designation: Open trailer (single axle) (standard commercial vehicle).

TRAILER
Anh. (1 achs.) mit geschl. Aufbau (o).

Net weight	200–300 kg	441–661 lb.
Pay load	300–500 kg	661–1,102 lb.
Gross weight	500–800 kg	1,102–1,764 lb.
Weight: axle	500–800 kg	1,102–1,764 lb.
Length (overall)	3,000 mm	9 ft., 10 ins.
Width (overall)	1,600 mm	5 ft., 3 ins.
Height (overall)	1,500 mm	4 ft., 11 ins.
Ground clearance	200 mm	7⅞ ins.
Tread centers	1,300 mm	4 ft. 3 ins.
Wheel width	120 mm	4¾ ins.
Angle of approach		
Angle of departure		
Fording depth		
Overturn gradient (crosswise)		45°

German nomenclature: Anhänger (1 achs.) mit geschlossenem Aufbau (o).

English designation: Trailer (single axle) with closed body (standard commercial vehicle).

TRAILER
Anh. (1 achs.) f. Mun. (Sd. Ah. 32)

Net weight	390 kg	860 lb.
Pay load	390 kg	860 lb.
Gross weight	780 kg	1,720 lb.
Weight: axle	780 kg	1,720 lb.
Length (overall)	2,160 mm	7 ft., 1 in.
Width (overall)	1,700 mm	5 ft., 7 ins.
Height (overall)	1,100 mm	3 ft., 7 ins.
Ground clearance	310 mm	12¼ ins.
Tread centers	1,446 mm	4 ft., 9 ins.
Wheel width	170 mm	6¾ ins.
Angle of approach		38°
Angle of departure		56°
Fording depth		
Overturn gradient (crosswise)		45°

German nomenclature: Anhänger (1 achs.) für Munition (Sd. Ah. 32).

English designation: Trailer (single axle) for ammunition.

TRAILER

Anh. (1 achs.) (Sd. Ah. 53)

Net weight	605 kg	1,334 lb.
Pay load	565 kg	1,245 lb.
Gross weight	1,170 kg	2,579 lb.
Weight: axle	1,170 kg	2,579 lb.
Length (overall)	3,250 mm	10 ft., 8 ins.
Width (overall)	1,825 mm	6 ft.
Height (overall)	1,570 mm	5 ft., 2 ins.
Ground clearance		
Tread centers	1,440 mm	4 ft., 9 ins.
Wheel width	170 mm	6¾ ins.
Angle of approach		
Angle of departure		
Fording depth		
Overturn gradient (crosswise)		

German nomenclature: Anhänger (1 achs.) (Sd. Ah. 53).

English designation: Trailer (single axle).

TRAILER

Anh. (1 achs.) f. Nb. W. Mun. (Sd. Ah. 33)

Net weight	340 kg	750 lb.
Pay load	360 kg	794 lb.
Gross weight	700 kg	1,543 lb.
Weight: axle	700 kg	1,543 lb.
Length (overall)	2,160 mm	7 ft., 1 in.
Width (overall)	1,700 mm	5 ft., 7 ins.
Height (overall)	1,110 mm	3 ft., 8 ins.
Ground clearance	310 mm	12¼ ins.
Tread centers	1,446 mm	4 ft., 9 ins.
Wheel width	170 mm	6¾ ins.
Angle of approach		
Angle of departure		45°
Fording depth		
Overturn gradient (crosswise)		45°

German nomenclature: Anhänger (1 achse) für Nebelwerfermunition (Sd. Ah. 33).

English designation: Trailer (single axle) for smoke ammunition.

SPECIAL TRAILER
Sd. Anh. (1 achs.) (Sd. Ah. 51)

Net weight	350 kg	772 lb.
Pay load	700 kg	1,543 lb.
Gross weight	1,050 kg	2,315 lb.
Weight: axle	1,050 kg	2,315 lb.
Length (overall)	2,520 mm	8 ft., 3 ins.
Width (overall)	1,810 mm	5 ft., 11 ins.
Height (overall)	1,100 mm	3 ft., 7 ins.
Ground clearance		
Tread centers	1,550 mm	5 ft., 1 in.
Wheel width	190 mm	7½ ins.
Angle of approach		
Angle of departure		
Fording depth		
Overturn gradient (crosswise)		

German nomenclature: Sonderanhänger (1 achs.)
(Sd. Ah. 51).

English designation: Special trailer (single axle) for
2 cm. AA guns.

TRAILER
Anh. (1 achs.) f. l. Lasten (Sd. Ah. 3)

Net weight	850 kg	1,874 lb.
Pay load	1,470 kg	3,240 lb.
Gross weight	2,320 kg	5,115 lb.
Weight: axle	2,320 kg	5,115 lb.
Length (overall)	2,370 mm	7 ft., 9 ins.
Width (overall)	2,300 mm	7 ft., 6 ins.
Height (overall)	1,400 mm	4 ft., 7 ins.
Ground clearance	275 mm	10⅞ ins.
Tread centers	2,050 mm	6 ft., 9 ins.
Wheel width	190 mm	7½ ins.
Angle of approach		
Angle of departure		
Fording depth		
Overturn gradient (crosswise)		

German nomenclature: Anhänger (1 achs.) für leichte
Lasten (Sd. Ah. 3).

English designation: Trailer (single axle) for light
loads.

SPECIAL TRAILER
Sd. Anh. (1 achs.) (Sd. Ah. 52)

Net weight	870 kg	1,918 lb.
Pay load	1,700 kg	3,747 lb.
Gross weight	2,570 kg	5,665 lb.
Weight: axle	2,570 kg	5,665 lb.
Length (overall)	3,500 mm	11 ft., 6 ins.
Width (overall)	2,420 mm	7 ft., 11 ins.
Height (overall)	1,320 mm	4 ft., 4 ins.
Ground clearance		
Tread centers	2,030 mm	6 ft., 8 ins.
Wheel width	190 mm	7½ ins.
Angle of approach		
Angle of departure		
Fording depth		
Overturn gradient (crosswise)		

German nomenclature: Sonderanhänger (1 achs.) (Sd. Ah. 52).

English designation: Special trailer 52 (single axle) for 2 cm AA guns.

TRAILER
nh. (1 achs.) f. m. od. s. Lasten (Sd. Ah. 4)

Net weight	1,500 kg	3,307 lb.
Pay load	3,300 kg	7,275 lb.
Gross weight	4,800 kg	10,582 lb.
Weight: axle	4,800 kg	10,582 lb.
Length (overall) (less ramps)	2,400 mm	7 ft., 10 ins.
Width (overall)	2,560 mm	8 ft., 5 ins.
Height (overall)	1,800 mm	5 ft., 11 ins.
Ground clearance	225 mm	8⅞ ins.
Tread centers	2,200 mm	7 ft., 3 ins.
Wheel width	270 mm	10⅝ ins.
Angle of approach		
Angle of departure		
Fording depth		
Overturn gradient (crosswise)		

German nomenclature: Anhänger (1 achs.) für mittlere oder schwere Lasten (Sd. Ah. 4).

English designation: Trailer (single axle) for medium or heavy loads.

TRAILER
Anh. (1 achs.) f. Fährsl. (Sd. Ah. 15)

German nomenclature: Anhänger (1 achs.) für Fährseil (Sd. Ah. 15).

English designation: Trailer (single axle) for ferry cable.

Net weight	550 kg	1,213 lb.
Pay load	300 kg	661 lb.
Gross weight	850 kg	1,874 lb.
Weight: axle	850 kg	1,874 lb.
Length (overall)	2,750 mm	9 ft.
Width (overall)	1,950 mm	6 ft., 5 ins.
Height (overall)	1,320 mm	4 ft., 4 ins.
Ground clearance	400 mm	15¾ ins.
Tread centers	1,650 mm	5 ft., 5 ins.
Wheel width	170 mm	6¾ ins.
Angle of approach		20°
Angle of departure		40°
Fording depth		
Overturn gradient (crosswise)		48°

TRAILER
Anh. (1 achs.) f. M. Boot (Sd. Ah. 13)

German nomenclature: Anhänger (1 achs.) für Motorboot (Sd. Ah. 13)

English designation: Trailer (single axle) for motorboat.

Net weight	2,000 kg	4,409 lb.
Pay load	2,200 kg	4,850 lb.
Gross weight	4,200 kg	9,258 lb.
Weight: axle	4,200 kg	9,259 lb.
Length (overall)	8,700 mm	28 ft., 7 ins.
Width (overall)	2,000 mm	6 ft., 7 ins.
Height (overall)	2,500 mm	8 ft., 2 ins.
Ground clearance	270 mm	10⅜ ins.
Tread centers	1,580 mm	5 ft., 2 ins.
Wheel width	270 mm	10⅝ ins.
Angle of approach		10°
Angle of departure		10°
Fording depth		
Overturn gradient (crosswise)		

TRAILER

Anh. (1 achs.) f. s. Langmat. (o)

Net weight	800 kg	1,764 lb.
Pay load	2,200 kg	4,850 lb.
Gross weight	3,000 kg	6,614 lb.
Weight: axle	3,000 kg	6,614 lb.
Length (overall)	2,000 mm	6 ft., 7 ins.
Width (overall)	2,200 mm	7 ft., 3 ins.
Height (overall)	2,400 mm	7 ft., 11 ins.
Ground clearance	450 mm	17¾ ins.
Tread centers	1,800 mm	5 ft., 11 ins.
Wheel width	435 mm	17 ins.
Angle of approach		
Angle of departure		
Fording depth		
Overturn gradient (crosswise)		

German nomenclature: Anhänger (1 achs.) für schweres Langmaterial (o).

English designation: Trailer (single axle) for heavy beams (standard commercial vehicle).

TRAILER

Anh. (1-od. mehrachs) f. Fsp. Bau (Sd. Ah. 21)

Net weight	800 kg	1,764 lb.
Pay load	3,700 kg	8,157 lb.
Gross weight	4,500 kg	9,921 lb.
Weight: Front axle	2,250 kg	4,960 lb.
Weight: Rear axle	2,250 kg	4,960 lb.
Length (overall)		
Width (overall)		
Height (overall)	1,770 mm	5 ft., 10 ins.
Ground clearance	400 mm	15¾ ins.
Tread centers	1,580 mm	5 ft., 2 ins.
Wheel width	210 mm	8¼ ins.
Angle of approach		
Angle of departure		
Fording depth		
Overturn gradient (lengthwise)		
Overturn gradient (crosswise)		40°
Turning radius		

German nomenclature: Anhänger (1-oder mehrachs) für Fernsprechbau (Sd. Ah. 21).

English designation: Trailer (one or more axles) for telephone construction.

TRAILER
Anh. (1 achs.) f. Erdkab. (Sd. Ah. 20)

German nomenclature: Anhänger (1 achs.) für Erdkabel (Sd. Ah. 20).

English designation: Trailer (single axle) for ground cable.

Net weight	560 kg	1,234 lb.
Pay load	980 kg	2,160 lb.
Gross weight	1,540 kg	3,394 lb.
Weight: axle	1,540 kg	3,394 lb.
Length (overall)	2,500 mm	8 ft., 2 ins.
Width (overall)	1,800 mm	5 ft., 11 ins.
Height (overall)	1,400 mm (approx.)	4 ft., 7 ins.
Ground clearance	380 mm	15 ins.
Tread centers	1,580 mm	5 ft., 2 ins.
Wheel width	190 mm	7½ ins.
Angle of approach		
Angle of departure		
Fording depth		
Overturn gradient (crosswise)		
TRAILER WITH CABEL, ROPE OR HOSE DRUMS		
Drum width	710 mm	28 ins.
Diameter (empty)	600 mm	23½ ins.
(full)	1,070 mm	42 ins.
Capacity	500 meters	1,640 ft.

TRANSPORTABLE GENERATOR
Masch. Satz. 220 V 6.5 kW als Anh. (1 achs.) fahrbar

German nomenclature: Maschinensatz 220 V 6.5 kW als Anhänger (1 achs.) fahrbar.

English designation: Transportable generator 220 V, 6.5 KW on trailer (single axle).

Net weight	1,450 kg	3,197 lb.
Pay load		
Gross weight	1,450 kg	3,197 lb.
Weight: axle	1,450 kg	3,197 lb.
Length (overall)	3,220 mm	10 ft., 6 ins.
Width (overall)	1,990 mm	6 ft., 6 ins.
Height (overall)	1,900 mm	6 ft., 3 ins.
Ground clearance	350 mm	13¾ ins.
Tread centers	1,530 mm	5 ft.
Wheel width	210 mm	8¼ ins.
Angle of approach		20°
Angle of departure		25°
Fording depth		
Overturn gradient (crosswise)		40°
POWER UNIT		
Piston displacement	1,500 cu cm	90 cu. ins.
Performance—horsepower	9 c–v	8.9 hp
Revolutions per minute		1,450
Type (cycles)		4
Capacity of fuel tank	75 liters	19.8 gal.
Fuel consumption per operating hour	6 liters	1.6 gal.
Total running time on one tank filling		12 hrs.
CURRENT GENERATOR (Electric Motor)		
Type of current		(direct current)
KW		6.5
Volt		220
Ampere		28.5

HEAVY TRANSPORTABLE GENERATOR A

Masch. Satz. A als Anh. (1 achs.) fahrbar (Sd. Ah. 24)

Net weight	2,050 kg	4,519 lb.
Gross weight	2,050 kg	4,519 lb.
Weight: axle	2,050 kg	4,519 lb.
Length (overall)	3,440 mm	11 ft., 3 ins.
Width (overall)	1,880 mm	6 ft., 2 ins.
Height (overall)	1,840 mm	6 ft.
Ground clearance	350 mm	13¾ ins.
Tread centers	1,500 mm	4 ft., 11 ins.
Wheel width	210 mm	8¼ ins.
Angle of approach		
Angle of departure		
Fording depth		
Overturn gradient (crosswise)		
POWER UNIT		
Piston displacement	2,496 cu cm	150 cu. ins.
Performance—horsepower	26 c–v	25.6 hp
Revolutions per minute		1,500
Type (cycles)		
Capacity of fuel tank	50 liters	13.2 gal.
Fuel consumption per operating hour	6.5 liters	1.7 gal.
Total running time on one tank filling		8 hrs.
CURRENT GENERATOR (Electric Motor)		
Type of current		(Three phase current)
Kilowatt		12
Volt		220/380
Ampere		25
Frequency		50

German nomenclature: schwerer Maschinensatz A als Anhänger (1 achse) fahrbar (Sd. Ah. 24).

English designation: Heavy transportable generator A on trailer (single axle).

TRANSPORTABLE GENERATOR

Masch. Satz 220/380 V (Drehstrom), etwa 30 kVA, als Anh. (1 achs.) fahrbar

Net weight	2,700 kg	5,952 lb.
Gross weight	2,750 kg	6,062 lb.
Weight: axle	2,700 kg	5,952 lb.
Length (overall)	4,300 mm	14 ft., 1 in.
Width (overall)	1,900 mm	6 ft., 3 ins.
Height (overall)	2,010 mm	6 ft., 7 ins.
Ground clearance	400 mm	15¾ ins.
Tread centers	1,800 mm	5 ft., 11 ins.
Wheel width	210 mm	8½ ins.
Angle of approach		
Angle of departure		
Fording depth		
Overturn gradient (crosswise)		
POWER UNIT		
Piston displacement	3,450 cu cm	207 cu. ins.
Performance—horsepower	40 c–v	39.5 hp
Revolutions per minute		1,500
Type (cycles)		4
Capacity of fuel tank	100 liters	26.4 gal.
Fuel consumption per operating hour	12.5 liters	3.3 gal.
Total running time on one tank filling		7–8 hrs.
CURRENT GENERATOR (Electric Motor)		
Type of current		(Three phase current
Kilowatt		30
Volt		220/380
Ampere		46
Frequency		50

German nomenclature: Maschinensatz 220/380 Volt (Drehstrom) etwa 30 kVA, als Anhänger (1 achse) fahrbar.

English designation: Transportable generator 220/280 volt (three phase current) approximately 30 kVA, on trailer (single axle).

TRANSPORTABLE GENERATOR
Masch. Satz. 110/220 V — etwa 24 kW als Anh. (1 achs.) fahrbar

German nomenclature: Maschinensatz 110/220 V—etwa 24 kW als Anhänger (1 achs.) fahrbar.

English designation: Transportable generator 110/220 V—approximately 24 KW on trailer (single axle).

Net weight	2,700 kg	5,962 lb.
Gross weight	2,700 kg	5,962 lb.
Weight: axle	2,700 kg	5,962 lb.
Length (overall)	4,110 mm	13 ft., 6 ins.
Width (overall)	1,840 mm	6 ft.
Height (overall)	1,850 mm	6 ft., 1 in.
Ground clearance	450 mm	17¾ ins.
Tread centers	1,520 mm	5 ft.
Wheel width	190 mm	7½ ins.
Angle of approach		
Angle of departure		
Fording depth		
Overturn gradient (crosswise)		
POWER UNIT		
Piston displacement	4,720 cu cm	283 cu. ins.
Performance—horsepower	48 to 50 c–v	47.3–49.3 hp
Revolutions per minute		1,450
Type (cycles)		4
Capacity of fuel tank	90 liters	23.8 gal.
Fuel consumption per operating hour	15 liters	4 gal.
Total running time on one tank filling		6
CURRENT GENERATOR (Electric Motor)		
Type of current		Direct current
Kilowatt		24
Volt		110/220
Ampere		218/109
Frequency		

TRANSPORTABLE MOTOR FIRE PUMP
Mot. Spr. als Anh. (1 achs.) fahrbar (o)

German nomenclature: Motorspritze als Anhänger (1 achs.) fahrbar (o).

English designation: Transportable motor fire pump on trailer (single axle) (standard commercial vehicle).

Net weight	750 kg	1,653 lb.
Gross weight	750 kg	1,653 lb.
Weight: axle	750 kg	1,653 lb.
Length (overall)	3,450 mm	11 ft., 4 ins.
Width (overall)	1,650 mm	5 ft., 5 ins.
Height (overall)	1,400 mm	4 ft., 7 ins.
Ground clearance	320 mm	12½ ins.
Tread centers	1,450 mm	4 ft., 9 ins.
Wheel width	170 mm	6¾ ins.
Angle of approach		
Angle of departure		
Fording depth		
Overturn gradient (crosswise)		45°
POWER UNIT		
Piston displacement	585 cu cm	35 cu. ins.
Performance—horsepower	14.5 c–v	14 hp
Revolutions per minute		2,900
Type (cycles)		2
Capacity of fuel tank	22 liters	5.8 gal.
Fuel consumption per operating hour	6 to 7 liters	1.6 to 1.8 gal.
Total running time on one tank filling		3
POWER DRIVEN SPRAY		
Capacity	400 to 600 l.p.m.	106–159 gal. p.m.
Pressure	10 atmosphere	147 lb. p.s.i.
Suction level	9.5 meters	31 ft., 2 ins.

RAILER

s. Anh. (1 achs.) (Ah. 301)

Net weight	670 kg	1,477 lb.
Pay load	580 kg	1,279 lb.
Gross weight	1,250 kg	2,756 lb.
Weight: axle	1,250 kg	2,756 lb.
Length (overall)	3,350 mm (approx.)	11 ft.
Width (overall)	1,880 mm	6 ft., 2 ins.
Height (overall)	1,825 mm	6 ft.
Ground clearance	260 mm	10¼ ins.
Tread centers	1,640 mm	5 ft., 4 ins.
Wheel width	190 mm	7½ ins.
Angle of approach		
Angle of departure		30°
Fording depth		
Overturn gradient (crosswise)		

erman nomenclature: Anhänger (1 achs.) für Tank-spritze (Ah. 301).

nglish designation: Trailer (single axle) for fire fighting water tank.

RAILER

gs. — Anh. (1 achs.) (o)

Net weight	850 kg	1,874 lb.
Gross weight	850 kg	1,874 lb.
Weight: axle	850 kg	1,874 lb.
Length (overall)	2,800 mm	9 ft., 2 ins.
Width (overall)	1,400 mm	4 ft., 7 ins.
Height (overall)	1,600 mm	5 ft., 3 ins.
Ground clearance	300 mm	11⅞ ins.
Tread centers	1,422 mm	4 ft., 8 ins.
Wheel width	190 mm	7½ ins.
Angle of approach		
Angle of departure		30°
Fording depth		
Overturn gradient (crosswise)		
POWER UNIT		
Piston displacement	909 cu cm	545 cu. ins.
Performance—horsepower	18 c–v	17.8 hp
Revolutions per minute		3,000
Type (cycles)		2
Capacity of fuel tank	30	7.9 gal.
Fuel consumption per operating hour	15	4 gal
Total running time on one tank filling		2 hrs.
TRAILER WITH CABLE ROPE OR HOSE DRUMS		
Drum width	960 mm	37¾ ins.
Diameter (empty)	100 mm	3⅞ ins.
(full)	450 mm	17¾ ins.
Capacity	75 mm	247 ft.
POWER DRIVEN SPRAY		
Capacity	800 l.p.m.	211 gal. p.m.
Pressure	8 cap.	118 lb. per sq. in.
Suction level	7.5 meters	24 ft., 7 ins.

erman nomenclature: Anhänger (1 achs.) für Trag-kraftspritze (o).

nglish designation: Trailer (single axle) for filling pump (standard commercial vehicle).

TRAILER
St. Anh. (1 achs.) (Ah. 302)

Net weight	650 kg	1,433 lb.
Pay load	710 kg	1,565 lb.
Gross weight	1,360 kg	2,998 lb.
Weight: axle	1,360 kg	2,998 lb.
Length (overall)	3,350 mm	11 ft.
Width (overall)	1,880 mm	6 ft., 2 ins.
Height (overall)	1,825 mm	6 ft.
Ground clearance	260 mm	10¼ ins.
Tread centers	1,640 mm	5 ft., 4 ins.
Wheel width	190 mm	7½ ins.
Angle of approach		
Angle of departure		30°
Fording depth		
Overturn gradient (crosswise)		

German nomenclature: Anhänger (1 achs.) für Schlauchtender (Ah. 302).

English designation: Trailer (single axle) for hose tender.

TRAILER
Anh. (1 achs.) f. Samml. Ger. D (Sd. Ah. 23)

Net weight	640 kg	1,411 lb.
Pay load	340 kg	750 kg
Gross weight	980 kg	2,161 lb.
Weight: axle	980 kg	2,161 lb.
Length (overall)	2,600 mm	8 ft., 6 ins.
Width (overall)	1,700 mm	5 ft., 7 ins.
Height (overall)	1,750 mm	5 ft., 9 ins.
Ground clearance	370 mm	14½ ins.
Tread centers	1,480 mm	4 ft., 10 ins.
Wheel width	210 mm	8¼ ins.
Angle of approach		
Angle of departure		
Fording depth		
Overturn gradient (crosswise)		
POWER UNIT		
Piston displacement	460 cu cm	27.6 cu. ins.
Performance—horsepower	6.2 c–v	6.1 hp
Revolutions per minute		2,000
Type (cycles)		2 (air cooled)
Capacity of fuel tank	16 liters	4.2 gal.
Fuel consumption per operating hour	2.5	.7 gal.
Total running time on one tank filling		7 hrs.
CURRENT GENERATOR (Electric Motor)		
Type of current		Direct current
Kilowatt		3.0
Volt		65
Ampere		46
Frequency		

German nomenclature: Anhänger (1 achs.) für Sammlerladegerät D (Sd. Ah. 23).

English designation: Trailer (single axle) for generator D.

ARGE AIR COMPRESSOR
. Druckl. Erz. 34 als Anh. (1 achs.) fahrbar

Net weight	850 kg	1,874 lb.
Pay load	1,050 kg	2,314 lb.
Gross weight	1,900 kg	4,188 lb.
Weight: axle	1,900 kg	4,188 lb.
Length (overall)	3,800 mm	12 ft., 5 ins.
Width (overall)	1,670 mm	5 ft., 6 ins.
Height (overall)	1,880 mm	6 ft., 2 ins.
Ground clearance	900 mm	35½ ins.
Tread centers	1,360 mm	4 ft., 5 ins.
Wheel width	210 mm	8¼ ins.
Angle of approach		30°
Angle of departure		60°
Fording depth		
Overturn gradient (crosswise)		45°
POWER UNIT		
Piston displacement	3,817 cu cm	229 cu. ins.
Performance—horsepower	39 c–v	38.5 hp
Revolutions per minute		1,500
Type (cycles)		4
Capacity of fuel tank	45	11.9 gal.
Fuel consumption per operating hour	7	1.8 gal.
Total running time on one tank filling		6½ hrs.
COMPRESSOR		
Capacity	3,000 l.p.m.	792 gal. p.m.
Pressure	6 atm.	88 lb. per sq. in.
Air tank capacity	200 liters	53 gal.

rman nomenclature: grosser Drucklufterzeuger 34
als Anhänger (1 achs.) fahrbar.

glish designation: Large air compressor 34 on trailer
(single axle).

OUGHKNEADING TRAILER
igknetanh. (1 achs.) (Sd. Ah. 35)

Net weight	1,100 kg	2,425 lb.
Gross weight	1,100 kg	2,425 lb.
Weight: axle	1,100 kg	2,425 lb.
Length (overall)	3,200 mm	10 ft., 6 ins.
Width (overall)	1,800 mm	5 ft., 11 ins.
Height (overall)	1,650 mm	5 ft., 5 ins.
Ground clearance	350 mm	13¾ ins.
Tread centers	1,530 mm	5 ft.
Wheel width	190 mm	7½ ins.
Angle of approach		20°
Angle of departure		25°
Fording depth		
Overturn gradient (crosswise)		35°
CURRENT GENERATOR (Electric Motor)		
Type of current		Direct current
Kilowatt		3.3
Volt		220
Ampere		19
Frequency		
DOUGHKNEADING MACHINE		
Capacity	150 kg dough	341 lb.
Power Unit		Electric motor
Capacity	1100	hr 1800 dough kg 3968 lb.

rman nomenclature: Teigknetanhänger (1 achs.)
(Sd. Ah. 35).

glish designation: Doughkneading trailer (single
xle).

DIRECTION AND RANGE FINDER TRAILER
Nav. Fupeil. Anh. (1 achs.) (Sd. Ah. 422)

German nomenclature: Navigations-Funkpeilanhänger
(1 achs.) (Sd. Ah. 422).

English designation: Direction and range finder trailer
(single axle).

Net weight	1,375 kg	3,031 lb.
Pay load	750 kg	1,654 lb.
Gross weight	2,125 kg	4,685 lb.
Weight: axle	2,125 kg	4,685 lb.
Length (overall)	4,200 mm	13 ft., 9 ins.
Width (overall)	1,860 mm	6 ft., 1 in.
Height (overall)	2,250 mm	6 ft., 9 ins.
Ground clearance	285 mm	11½ ins.
Tread centers	1,560 mm	5 ft., 1 in.
Wheel width	190 mm	7½ ins.
Angle of approach		15°
Angle of departure		25°
Seating capacity		4
Fording depth		
Overturn gradient (crosswise)		

SPECIAL TRAILER
Sd. Anh. (1 achs.) (Sd. Ah. 55)

German nomenclature: Sonderanhänger (1 achs.)
(Sd. Ah. 65).

English designation: Special trailer (single axle).

Net weight	1,150 kg	2,535 lb.
Pay load	650 kg	1,433 lb.
Gross weight	1,800 kg	3,968 lb.
Weight: axle	1,800 kg	3,968 lb.
Length (overall)	3,200 mm	10 ft., 6 ins.
Width (overall)	2,000 mm	6 ft., 7 ins.
Height (overall)	2,620 mm	8 ft., 7 ins.
Ground clearance	300 mm	11⅞ ins.
Tread centers	1,700 mm	5 ft., 7 ins.
Wheel width	200 mm	7⅞ ins.
Angle of approach		25°
Angle of departure		25°
Seating capacity		
Fording depth		
Overturn gradient (crosswise)		45°

PECIAL TRAILER
1. Anh. (1 achs.) (Sd. Ah. 54)

Net weight	800 kg	1,764 lb.
Pay load	450 kg	992 lb.
Gross weight	1,250 kg	2,756 lb.
Weight: axle	1,250 kg	2,756 lb.
Length (overall)	3,250 mm	10 ft., 8 ins.
Width (overall)	1,825 mm	6 ft.
Height (overall)	1,570 mm	5 ft., 2 ins.
Ground clearance	300 mm	11⅞ ins.
Tread centers	1,140 mm	4 ft., 8 ins.
Wheel width	170 mm	6¾ ins.
Angle of approach		25°
Angle of departure		25°
Seating capacity		
Fording depth		
Overturn gradient (crosswise)		50°

rman nomenclature: Sonderanhänger (1 achs) Sd. Ah. 54).

glish designation: Special trailer (single axle).

ESEL ENGINE ICE MAKER
eseleisber. 40 Anh. (1 achs.) fahrbar

Net weight	3,270 kg	7,209 lb.
Pay load	1,350 kg	2,965 lb.
Gross weight	4,620 kg	10,174 lb.
Weight: Front axle		
Length (overall)	4,740 mm	15 ft., 7 ins.
Width (overall)	2,260 mm	7 ft., 5 ins.
Height (overall)	2,510 mm	8 ft., 3 ins.
Ground clearance	240 mm	9½ ins.
Tread centers	1,240 mm	4 ft., 1 in.
Wheel width		
Angle of approach		
Angle of departure		
Seating capacity		
Fording depth		
Overturn gradient (crosswise)		

rman nomenclature: Dieseleisbereiter 40 als An-änger (1 achs.) fahrbar.

lish designation: Transportable diesel engine ice aker 40 on trailer (single axle).

LARGE REFRIGERATION TRAILER
Gr. Kühlb. Anh. (Sd. Ah. 107)

German nomenclatutre: Grosskühlbehälteranhänger (Sd. Ah. 107).

English designation: Large refrigeration trailer.

Net weight		
Pay load		
Gross weight		
Weight: axle	2,000 kg	4,409 lb.
Length (overall)	4,650 mm	15 ft., 3 ins.
Width (overall)	2,260 mm	7 ft., 5 ins.
Height (overall)	2,575 mm	8 ft., 5 ins.
Ground clearance	320 mm	12½ ins.
Tread centers		
Wheel width		
Angle of approach		
Angle of departure		
Seating capacity		
Fording depth		
Overturn gradient (crosswise)........		
POWER UNIT		
Piston displacement	4000 cu cm	240 cu. ins.
Performance—horsepower		
Revolutions per minute		
Type (cycles)		
Capacity of fuel tank		
Fuel consumption per operating hour		
Total running time on one tank filling		

TRAILER, OPEN
Anh. (mehrachs.) off (o)

German nomenclature: Anhänger (mehrachs.) offen (o).

English designation: Trailer (multiple axle) open (standard commercial vehicle).

Net weight	5,000 kg	11,023 lb.
Pay load	11,000 kg	24,250 lb.
Gross weight	16,000 kg	35,270 lb.
Weight: Front axle	5,000 kg	11,023 lb.
Weight: Rear axle	5,500 kg	12,125 lb.
Length (overall)	7,789 mm	25 ft., 7 ins.
Width (overall)	2,360 mm	7 ft., 9 ins.
Height (overall)	1,970 mm	6 ft., 6 ins.
Ground clearance	500 mm	19⅞ ins.
Tread centers	1,830 mm	6 ft.
Wheelbase	4,950/1,230 mm	195/49 ins.
Wheel width	300 mm	11⅞ ins.
Angle of approach		90°
Angle of departure		45°
Seating capacity		
Fording depth		
Overturn gradient (lengthwise)......		
Overturn gradient (crosswise)........		
Turning radius		

TRAILER

Ah. (mehrachs.) mit geschl. Aufbau (o)

Net weight	3,500 kg	7,716 lb.
Pay load	7,500 kg	16,534 lb.
Gross weight	11,000 kg	24,250 lb.
Weight: Front axle	5,500 kg	11,125 lb.
Weight: Rear axle	5,500 kg	11,125 lb.
Length (overall)	7,900 mm	25 ft., 11 ins.
Width (overall)	2,350 mm	7 ft., 8 ins.
Height (overall)	3,100 mm	10 ft., 2 ins.
Ground clearance	250 mm	9⅞ ins.
Tread centers	1,560 mm	5 ft., 1 in.
	1,900 mm	6 ft., 3 ins.
Wheelbase	4,200 mm	13 ft., 9 ins.
Wheel width	255 mm	10 ins.
Angle of approach		90°
Angle of departure		35°
Seating capacity		
Fording depth		
Overturn gradient (lengthwise)		
Overturn gradient (crosswise)		
Turning radius		

German nomenclature: Anhänger (mehrachs.) mit geschloffenem Aufbau (o).

English designation: Trailer (multiple axle) with closed body (standard commercial vehicle).

TRAILER

Ah. (mehrachs.) f. mod. s. Lasten (Sd. Ah. 103)

Net weight	1,200 kg	2,645 lb.
Pay load	3,200 kg	7,055 lb.
Gross weight	4,400 kg	9,700 lb.
Weight: Front axle	2,200 kg	4,850 lb.
Weight: Rear axle	2,200 kg	4,850 lb.
Length (overall)	2,920 mm	9 ft., 7 ins.
Width (overall)	2,400 mm	7 ft., 10 ins.
Height (overall)	1,300 mm	4 ft., 3 ins.
Ground clearance	325 mm	12¾ ins.
Tread centers	2,150 mm	7 ins.
Wheelbase		
Wheel width	190 mm	7½ ins.
Angle of approach		
Angle of departure		
Fording depth		
Overturn gradient (lengthwise)		
Overturn gradient (crosswise)		
Turning radius		

German nomenclature: Anhänger (mehrachs.) für mittlere oder schwere Lasten (Sd. Ah. 103).

English designation: Trailer (multiple axle) for medium or heavy loads.

MEDIUM TRAILER WITH FUEL TANK
m. Anh. mit Betr. St. Kess. Anl. (o)

German nomenclature: mittlerer Anhänger mit Betriebestoffkesselenlage (o).

English designation: Medium trailer with fuel tank (standard commercial vehicle).

Net weight	3,300 kg	7,275 lb.
Pay load	2,200 kg	4,850 lb.
Gross weight	5,700 kg	12,566 lb.
Weight: Front axle	2,800 kg	6,173 lb.
Weight: Rear axle	2,900 kg	6,393 lb.
Length (overall)	4,800 mm	15 ft., 9 ins.
Width (overall)	2,050 mm	6 ft., 9 ins.
Height (overall)	2,650 mm	8 ft., 8 ins.
Ground clearance	180 mm	$7\frac{1}{8}$ ins.
Tread centers	1,500 mm	4 ft., 11 ins.
Wheelbase		
Wheel width	230 mm	9 ins.
Angle of approach		45°
Angle of departure		45°
Seating capacity		
Fording depth		
Overturn gradient (lengthwise)		
Overturn gradient (crosswise)		
Turning radius		

HEAVY TRAILER WITH FUEL TANK
s. Anh. mit Betr. St. Kess. Anl. (o)

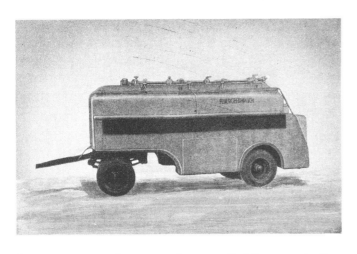

German nomenclature: schwerer Anhänger mit Betriebsstoffkesselanlage (o).

English designation: Heavy trailer with fuel tank (standard commercial vehicle).

Net weight	5,300 kg	11,684 lb.
Pay load	5,100 kg	11,243 lb.
Gross weight	10,400 kg	22,121 lb.
Weight: Front axle	4,000 kg	8,818 lb.
Weight: Rear axle	6,400 kg	14,109 lb.
Length (overall)	7,750 mm	25 ft., 5 ins.
Width (overall)	2,400 mm	7 ft., 10 ins.
Height (overall)	2,730 mm	8 ft., 11 ins.
Ground clearance	330 mm	13 ins.
Tread centers	1,970 mm	6 ft., 5 ins.
Wheelbase	3,350 mm	132 ins.
Wheel width	450 mm	$17\frac{3}{4}$ ins.
Angle of approach		70°
Angle of departure		15°
Seating capacity		
Fording depth		
Overturn gradient (lengthwise)		
Overturn gradient (crosswise)		
Turning radius		

AIRPLANE FUEL TANK TRAILER
o. K. Anh. (Ah. 454)

Net weight	4,200 kg	9,258 lb.
Pay load	2,625 kg	5,787 lb.
Gross weight	6,825 kg	15,045 lb.
Weight: Front axle	3,000 kg	6,614 lb.
Weight: Rear axle	3,825 kg	8,432 lb.
Length (overall)	6,750 mm	22 ft., 2 ins.
Width (overall)	2,500 mm	8 ft., 2 ins.
Height (overall)	2,070 mm	6 ft., 9 ins.
Ground clearance	230 mm	9 ins.
Tread centers	2,000 mm	6 ft., 7 ins.
Wheelbase	2,850 mm	112 ins.
Wheel width	230 mm	9 ins.
Angle of approach		
Angle of departure		
Seating capacity		
Fording depth		
Overturn gradient (lengthwise)		
Overturn gradient (crosswise)		
Turning radius		

German nomenclature: Flugbetriebsstoff-Kesselwagen als Anhänger (Ah. 454).

English designation: Airplane fuel tank trailer.

FIELD OVEN
Backanh. (Sd. Ah. 105)

Net weight	1,900 kg	4,188 lb.
Gross weight	1,900 kg	4,188 lb.
Weight: Front axle	750 kg	1,653 lb.
Weight: Rear axle	1,150 kg	2,535 lb.
Length (overall)	3,760 mm	12 ft., 4 ins.
Width (overall)	1,900 mm	6 ft., 3 ins.
Height (overall)	2,100 mm	6 ft., 11 ins.
Ground clearance	320 mm	12⅝ ins.
Tread centers	1,530 mm	5 ft.
Wheelbase	1,950 mm	77 ins.
Wheel width	190 mm	7½ ins.
Angle of approach		55°
Angle of departure		40°
Seating capacity		
Fording depth		
Overturn gradient (lengthwise)		
Overturn gradient (crosswise)		35°
Turning radius		

German nomenclature: Backanhänger (Sd. Ah. 105).

English designation: Field oven.

FIELD OVEN
Backanh. (Sd. Ah. 106).

German nomenclature: Backanhänger (Sd. Ah. 106).

English designation: Field oven.

Net weight	2,835 kg	6,250 lb.
Gross weight	2,835 kg	6,250 lb.
Weight: Front axle	1,200 kg	2,645 lb.
Weight: Rear axle	1,635 kg	3,604 lb.
Length (overall)	3,700 mm	13 ft.
Width (overall)	2,000 mm	6 ft., 7 ins.
Height (overall)	2,200 mm	7 ft., 3 ins.
Ground clearance	400 mm	15¾ ins.
Tread centers	1,650 mm	5 ft., 5 ins.
Wheelbase	1,145 mm	45 ins.
Wheel width	190 mm	7½ ins.
Angle of approach		70°
Angle of departure		35
Seating capacity		
Fording depth		
Overturn gradient (lengthwise)		
Overturn gradient (crosswise)		30°
Turning radius		
BAKERY TRAILER		
Type of heating		Wood and C
Consumption of fuel kg		7.5
Cap. per 2 hr. 160 loaves		

LIGHT GENERATOR TRAILER
Bel. Anh. (Ah. 51)

German nomenclature: Beleuchtungsanhänger (Ah. 51).

English designation: Light generator trailer.

Net weight	2,680 kg	5,908 lb.
Pay load	2,000 kg	4,409 lb.
Gross weight	4,680 kg	10,317 lb.
Weight: Front axle	1,872 kg	4,127 lb.
Weight: Rear axle	2,808 kg	6,191 lb.
Length (overall)	5,500 mm	18 ft.
Width (overall)	2,000 mm	6 ft., 7 ins.
Height (overall)	3,000 mm	9 ft., 10 ins.
Ground clearance	250 mm	9⅞ ins.
Tread centers		
Wheelbase	2,000 mm	79 ins.
Wheel width	190 mm	7½ ins.
Angle of approach		40°
Angle of departure		65°
Seating capacity		2
Fording depth		
Overturn gradient (lengthwise)		45°
Overturn gradient (crosswise)		35°
Turning radius		
POWER UNIT		
Piston displacement	1,300 cu cm	78 cu. ins.
Performance—horsepower	17 c–v	16.8 hp
Revolutions per minute		1,700
Type (cycles)		4
Capacity of fuel tank	65 liters	17.2 gal.
Fuel consumption per operating hour	10	2.64 gal.
Total running time on one tank filling		5½
CURRENT GENERATOR (Electric Motor)		
Type of current		Direct curren
Kilowatt		6
Volt		220
Ampere		6 to 25
Frequency		

EDIUM BEACON TRAILER
Leu. Feu. Anh. (2 achs.) (Ah. 473)

rman nomenclature: mittlerer Leuchtfeueranhänger 2 achs.) (Ah. 473).

glish designation: Medium beacon trailer (twin xled).

Net weight	3,115 kg	6,867 lb.
Pay load	1,385 kg	3,054 lb.
Gross weight	4,500 kg	9,921 lb.
Weight: Front axle	2,100 kg	4,630 lb.
Weight: Rear axle	2,400 kg	5,292 lb.
Length (overall)	5,540 mm	18 ft., 2 ins.
Width (overall)	2,120 mm	6 ft., 11 ins.
Height (overall)	2,915 mm	9 ft., 7 ins.
Ground clearance	200 mm	7⅞ ins.
Tread centers	1,580 mm	5 ft., 2 ins.
Wheelbase	2,250 mm	88 ins.
Wheel width	190 mm	7½ ins.
Angle of approach		
Angle of departure		
Seating capacity		5
Fording depth		
Overturn gradient (lengthwise)		
Overturn gradient (crosswise)		
Turning radius		

ELETYPE CONNECTION TRAILER
chrb. Anschl. Anh. (2 achs.) (Ah. 469)

man nomenclature: Fernschreib-Anschlussanhänger 2 achs.) (Ah. 469).

lish designation: Teletype connection trailer (twin xled).

Net weight	2,520 kg	5,556 lb.
Pay load	1,230 kg	2,705 lb.
Gross weight	3,750 kg	8,261 lb.
Weight: Front axle	1,500 kg	3,307 lb.
Weight: Rear axle	2,250 kg	4,960 lb.
Length (overall)	6,800 mm	22 ft., 4 ins.
Width (overall)	2,100 mm	6 ft., 11 ins.
Height (overall)	3,100 mm	10 ft., 2 ins.
Ground clearance	250 mm	9⅞ ins.
Tread centers	1,600 mm	5 ft., 3 ins.
Wheelbase	2,835 mm	111 ins.
Wheel width	190 mm	7½ ins.
Angle of approach		
Angle of departure		
Seating capacity		4
Fording depth		
Overturn gradient (lengthwise)		
Overturn gradient (crosswise)		
Turning radius		

TELEPHONE EXCHANGE TRAILER
Fsp. Verm. Anh. (2 achs.) (Ah. 468)

German nomenclature: Fernsprech-Vermittlungsan-
hänger (2 achs.) (Ah. 468).

English designation: Telephone exchange trailer (twin
axled).

Net weight	3,360 kg	7,407 lb.
Pay load	2,120 kg	4,673 lb.
Gross weight	5,480 kg	12,080 lb.
Weight: Front axle	2,440 kg	5,380 lb.
Weight: Rear axle	3,040 kg	6,702 lb.
Length (overall)	6,800 mm	22 ft., 4 ins.
Width (overall)	2,400 mm	7 ft., 10½ ins
Height (overall)	1,800 mm	5 ft., 11 ins.
Ground clearance	300 mm	11⅞ ins.
Tread centers	1,820 mm	6 ft.
	2,060 mm	6 ft., 9 ins.
Wheelbase		
Wheel width		
Angle of approach		
Angle of departure		
Seating capacity		10
Fording depth		
Overturn gradient (lengthwise)		
Overturn gradient (crosswise)		
Turning radius		

RADIO TRAILER
Fu. Anh. (Kzw/Lgw) (2 achs.) (Ah. 470)

German nomenclature: Funkanhänger (Kurzwelle/
Langwelle) (2 achs.) (Ah. 470).

English designation: Radio trailer (long or short wave)
(twin axled).

Net weight	3,200 kg	7,055 lb.
Pay load	400 kg	882 lb.
Gross weight	3,600 kg	7,937 lb.
Weight: Front axle	1,650 kg	3,638 lb.
Weight: Rear axle	1,950 kg	4,298 lb.
Length (overall)	5,480 mm	18 ft.
Width (overall)	2,070 mm	6 ft., 9 ins.
Height (overall)	2,960 mm	9 ft., 9 ins.
Ground clearance	200 mm	7⅞ ins.
Tread centers	1,580 mm	5 ft., 2 ins.
Wheelbase	2,250 mm	7 ft., 4 ins.
Wheel width	190 mm	7½ ins.
Angle of approach		
Angle of departure		
Seating capacity		5
Fording depth		
Overturn gradient (lengthwise)		
Overturn gradient (crosswise)		
Turning radius		

IGHT BEACON TRAILER

Leu. Feu.-Anh. (2 achs.) (Ah. 472)

rman nomenclature: leichter Leuchtfeueranhänger
(2 achs.) (Ah. 472).

glish designation: Light beacon trailer (twin axled).

Net weight	3,115 kg	6,867 lb.
Pay load	1,385 kg	3,054 lb.
Gross weight	4,500 kg	9,921 lb.
Weight: Front axle	2,100 kg	4,630 lb.
Weight: Rear axle	2,400 kg	5,292 lb.
Length (overall)	5,540 mm	18 ft., 2 ins.
Width (overall)	2,120 mm	6 ft., 11 ins.
Height (overall)	2,915 mm	9 ft., 7 ins.
Ground clearance	200 mm	7⅞ ins.
Tread centers	1,580 mm	5 ft., 2 ins.
Wheelbase	2,250 mm	88 ins.
Wheel width	190 mm	7½ ins.
Angle of approach		
Angle of departure		
Seating capacity		5
Fording depth		
Overturn gradient (lengthwise)		
Overturn gradient (crosswise)		
Turning radius		

ADIO EXCHANGE OFFICE TRAILER

tr. Fu. Empf. Anh. (2 achs.) (Ah. 471)

rman nomenclature: Betriebs-Funkempfangsan-
änger (2 achs.) (Ah. 471).

glish designation: Radio exchange office trailer
(twin axle).

Net weight	3,100 kg	6,834 lb.
Pay load	500 kg	1,103 lb.
Gross weight	3,600 kg	7,937 lb.
Weight: Front axle	1,650 kg	3,638 lb.
Weight: Rear axle	1,950 kg	4,298 lb.
Length (overall)	5,600 mm	18 ft., 4 ins.
Width (overall)	2,100 mm	6 ft., 11 ins.
Height (overall)	2,950 mm	9 ft., 8 ins.
Ground clearance	200 mm	7⅞ ins.
Tread centers	1,580 mm	5 ft., 2 ins.
Wheelbase	2,250 mm	7 ft., 4 ins.
Wheel width	190 mm	7½ ins.
Angle of approach		20°
Angle of departure		25°
Seating capacity		6
Fording depth		
Overturn gradient (lengthwise)		
Overturn gradient (crosswise)		
Turning radius		

DIRECTION OR RANGE FINDER TRAILER
Nav. Fupeil-Anh. (2 achs.) (Ah. 447)

German nomenclature: Navigations-Funkpeilanhänger (2 achs.) (Ah. 447).

English designation: Direction or range finder trailer (twin axled).

Net weight	2,737 kg	6,034 lb.
Pay load	1,513 kg	3,333 lb.
Gross weight	4,250 kg	9,367 lb.
Weight: Front axle	2,050 kg	4,519 lb.
Weight: Rear axle	2,200 kg	4,850 lb.
Length (overall)	5,540 mm	18 ft., 2 ins.
Width (overall)	2,120 mm	6 ft., 11 ins.
Height (overall)	2,915 mm	9 ft., 7 ins.
Ground clearance	200 mm	7⅞ ins.
Tread centers	1,580 mm	5 ft., 2¼ ins.
Wheelbase		
Wheel width	190 mm	7½ ins.
Angle of approach		20°
Angle of departure		25°
Seating capacity		5
Fording depth		
Overturn gradient (lengthwise)		
Overturn gradient (crosswise)		
Turning radius		

HEAVY SURVEYING TRAILER
s. Verm. Anh. (Sd. Ah. III)

German nomenclature: schwerer Vermessungsanhänger (Sd. Ah. III).

English designation: Heavy surveying trailer.

Net weight	6,100 kg	13,448 lb.
Pay load	4,400 kg	9,700 lb.
Gross weight	10,700 kg	23,583 lb.
Weight: Front axle	5,350 kg	11,792 lb.
Weight: Rear axle	5,350 kg	11,792 lb.
Length (overall)	9,100 mm	29 ft., 10 ins.
Width (overall)	2,500 mm	8 ft., 2 ins.
Height (overall)	3,060 mm	10 ft.
Ground clearance	250 mm	9⅞ ins.
Tread centers	1,650 mm	5 ft., 5 ins.
Wheelbase	5,500 mm	18 ft.
Wheel width	208 mm	8 ins.
Angle of approach		
Angle of departure		
Seating capacity		
Fording depth		
Overturn gradient (lengthwise)		
Overturn gradient (crosswise)		
Turning radius		

TRAILER FOR PLANE WINGS
Tragfl. Anh. 6 m (Sd. Anh. 450)

Net weight	1,700 kg	3,747 lb.
Pay load	500 kg	1,103 lb.
Gross weight	2,200 kg	4,850 lb.
Weight: Front axle	1,100 kg	2,425 lb.
Weight: Rear axle	1,100 kg	2,425 lb.
Length (overall)	8,300 mm	27 ft., 3 ins.
Width (overall)	1,800 mm	5 ft., 11 ins.
Height (overall)	3,000 mm	9 ft., 10 ins.
Ground clearance	260 mm	10¼ ins.
Tread centers	1,500 mm	4 ft., 11 ins.
Wheelbase	4,610 mm	15 ft., 2 ins.
Wheel width	190 mm	7½ ins.
Angle of approach		
Angle of departure		
Fording depth		
Overturn gradient (lengthwise)		
Overturn gradient (crosswise)		
Turning radius		

German nomenclature: Anhänger für Tragflächen, 6 meters (Sd. Ah. 450).

English designation: Trailer for plane wings, 6 meters.

TRAILER FOR AIRPLANE WINGS
Tragfl. Anh. 10 m (Sd. Ah. 451)

Net weight	2,400 kg	5,292 lb.
Pay load		
Gross weight	3,400 kg	7,496 lb.
Weight: Front axle	1,700 kg	3,747 lb.
Weight: Rear axle	1,700 kg	3,747 lb.
Length (overall)	11,000 mm	36 ft., 1 in.
Width (overall)	1,900 mm	6 ft., 3 ins.
Height (overall)	3,800 mm	12 ft., 6 ins.
Ground clearance	260 mm	10¼ ins.
Tread centers	1,700 mm	
Wheelbase		
Wheel width	190 mm	
Angle of approach		
Angle of departure		
Fording depth		
Overturn gradient (lengthwise)		
Overturn gradient (crosswise)		
Turning radius		

German nomenclature: Anhänger für Tragflächen 10 meters (Sd. Ah. 451).

English designation: Trailer for airplane wings, 10 meters.

SPECIAL TRAILER
Sd. Anh. 104

German nomenclature: Sonderanhänger 104.

English designation: Special trailer 104.

Net weight	1,830 kg	4,034 lb.
Pay load	2,500 kg	5,512 lb.
Gross weight	4,330 kg	9,546 lb.
Weight: Front axle	2,165 kg	4,773 lb.
Weight: Rear axle	2,165 kg	4,773 lb.
Length (overall)	6,500 mm	21 ft., 4 ins.
Width (overall)	2,135 mm	7 ft.
Height (overall)	1,100 mm	3 ft., 7 ins.
Ground clearance		
Tread centers	1,700 mm	5 ft., 7 ins.
Wheelbase		Variable
Wheel width	210 mm	8¼ ins.
Angle of approach		
Angle of departure		
Fording depth		
Overturn gradient (lengthwise)		
Overturn gradient (crosswise)		
Turning radius		

SPECIAL TRAILER
Sd. Anh. 201

German nomenclature: Sonderanhänger 201.

English designation: Special trailer 201.

Net weight	1,970 kg	4,342 lb.
Pay load		
Gross weight	7,370 kg	16,247 lb.
Weight: Front axle	2,570 kg	5,666 lb.
Weight: Rear axle	4,800 kg	10,582 lb.
Length (overall)	6,200 mm	20 ft., 4 ins.
Width (overall)	2,300 mm	7 ft., 6½ ins.
Height (overall)	1,220 mm	4 ft.
Ground clearance		
Tread centers	1,770 mm	5 ft., 10 ins.
	1,750 mm	5 ft., 9 ins.
Wheelbase		Variable accor- ing to equi- ment
Wheel width	210 mm	8¼ ins.
Angle of approach		
Angle of departure		
Seating capacity		
Fording depth		
Overturn gradient (lengthwise)		
Overturn gradient (crosswise)		
Turning radius		

SPECIAL TRAILER
Sd. Anh. 202

German nomenclature: Sonderanhänger 202.

English designation: Special trailer 202.

Net weight	3,200 kg	7,055 lb.
Pay load	6,000 kg	13,233 lb.
Gross weight	9,200 kg	20,288 lb.
Weight: Front axle	4,600 kg	10,144 lb.
Weight: Rear axle	4,600 kg	10,144 lb.
Length (overall)	1,000 mm	3 ft., 3 ins.
Width (overall)	2,400 mm	7 ft., 10 ins.
Height (overall)	1,250 mm	4 ft., 1 in.
Ground clearance		
Tread centers	1,850 mm	6 ft., 1 in.
Wheelbase		Variable according to equipment
Wheel width	210 mm	8¼ ins.
Angle of approach		
Angle of departure		
Seating capacity		
Fording depth		
Overturn gradient (lengthwise)		
Overturn gradient (crosswise)		
Turning radius		

SPECIAL TRAILER
Sd. Anh. 203

German nomenclature: Sonderanhänger 203.

English designation: Special trailer 203.

Net weight	4,500 kg	9,921 lb.
Pay load	10,000 kg	22,045 lb.
Gross weight	14,500 kg	31,966 lb.
Weight: Front axle	7,250 kg	15,983 lb.
Weight: Rear axle	7,250 kg	15,983 lb.
Length (overall)	9,000 mm	29 ft., 6 ins.
Width (overall)	2,470 mm	8 ft., 1 in.
Height (overall)	1,250 mm	4 ft., 1 in.
Ground clearance		
Tread centers	1,935 mm	6 ft., 4 ins.
Wheelbase		Variable according to equipment
Wheel width	210 mm	8¼ ins.
Angle of approach		
Angle of departure		
Seating capacity		
Fording depth		
Overturn gradient (lengthwise)		
Overturn gradient (crosswise)		
Turning radius		

SPECIAL TRAILER
Sd. Anh. 204

German nomenclature: Sonderanhänger 204.

English designation: Special trailer 204.

Net weight	2,375 kg	5,236 lb.
Pay load	4,500 kg	9,920 lb.
Gross weight	6,875 kg	15,156 lb.
Weight: Front axle	3,440 kg	7,584 lb.
Weight: Rear axle	3,435 kg	7,573 lb.
Length (overall)	6,500 mm	21 ft., 4 ins.
Width (overall)	2,350 mm	7 ft., 8 ins.
Height (overall)	1,400 mm	4 ft., 7 ins.
Ground clearance		
Tread centers	2,000 mm	6 ft., 7 ins.
	2,000 mm	6 ft., 7 ins.
Wheelbase		Variable according to equipment
Wheel width	210 mm	8¼ ins.
Angle of approach		
Angle of departure		
Seating capacity		
Fording depth		
Overturn gradient (lengthwise)		
Overturn gradient (crosswise)		
Turning radius		

TRAILER FOR ASSAULT BOAT
Anh. für Sturmb. (Sd. Ah. 108)

German nomenclature: Anhänger für Sturmboot (Sd. Ah. 108)

English designation: Trailer for assault boat.

Net weight	1,450 kg	3,196 lb.
Pay load	1,550 kg	3,417 lb.
Gross weight	3,000 kg	6,614 lb.
Weight: Front axle	1,250 kg	2,756 lb.
Weight: Rear axle	1,750 kg	3,857 lb.
Length (overall)	7,435 mm	24 ft., 5 ins.
Width (overall)	2,000 mm	6 ft., 7 ins.
Height (overall)	2,200 mm	7 ft., 3 ins.
Ground clearance	290 mm	11⅝ ins.
Tread centers	1,730 mm	5 ft., 8 ins.
Wheelbase	3,600 mm	142 ins.
Wheel width	170 mm	6¾ ins.
Angle of approach		32°
Angle of departure		25°
Seating capacity		
Fording depth		
Overturn gradient (lengthwise)		67°
Overturn gradient (crosswise)		37°
Turning radius		

LIGHT SUPPORTING TRAILER
Bockw. (Pf. 14)

Net weight	1,700 kg	3,747 lb.
Pay load	3,000 kg	6,614 lb.
Gross weight	4,700 kg	10,361 lb.
Weight: Front axle	2,350 kg	5,181 lb.
Weight: Rear axle	2,350 kg	5,181 lb.
Length (overall)	9,050 mm	29 ft., 8 ins.
Width (overall)	2,050 mm	6 ft., 9 ins.
Ground clearance	330 mm	13 ins.
Tread centers	1,700 mm	5 ft., 10 ins.
Wheelbase	4,000 mm	157 ins.
Wheel width	215 mm	8½ ins.
Angle of approach		28°
Angle of departure		25°
Seating capacity		
Fording depth		
Overturn gradient (lengthwise)		
Overturn gradient (crosswise)		35°
Turning radius		

German nomenclature: leichter Bockwagen (Pf. 14).

English designation: Light supporting trailer or semi-trailer.

BOX CAR TRAILER
Bockw. (Pf. 8)

Net weight	1,378 kg	3,038 lb.
Pay load	1,756 kg	3,870 lb.
Gross weight	3,134 kg	6,909 lb.
Weight: Front axle	1,527 kg	3,367 lb.
Weight: Rear axle	1,607 kg	3,542 lb.
Length (overall)	8,080 mm	26 ft., 6 ins.
Width (overall)	1,960 mm	6 ft., 5 ins.
Height (overall)	1,600 mm	5 ft., 3 ins.
Ground clearance	400 mm	15¾ ins.
Tread centers	1,530 mm	5 ft.
Wheelbase	3,510 mm	138 ins.
Wheel width	165 mm	6½ ins.
Angle of approach		32°
Angle of departure		34°
Fording depth		
Overturn gradient (lengthwise)		
Overturn gradient (crosswise)		32°
Turning radius		

German nomenclature: Bockwagen (Pf. 8).

English designation: Box car trailer or semi-trailer.

111

BOX CAR TRAILER
Bockw. (Pf. 10)

German nomenclature: Bockwagen (Pf. 10).

English designation: Box car trailer or semi-trailer.

Net weight	2,050 kg	4,519 lb.
Pay load	2,850 kg	6,283 lb.
Gross weight	4,900 kg	10,802 lb.
Weight: Front axle	2,400 kg	5,292 lb.
Weight: Rear axle	2,500 kg	5,512 lb.
Length (overall)	8,650 mm	28 ft., 4 ins.
Width (overall)	2,150 mm	7 ft.
Height (overall)	2,000 mm	6 ft., 7 ins.
Ground clearance	350 mm	13¾ ins.
Tread centers	1,610 mm	5 ft., 3 ins.
Wheelbase	3,615 mm	142 ins.
Wheel width	370 mm	14⅝ ins.
Angle of approach		30°
Angle of departure		28°
Seating capacity		
Fording depth		
Overturn gradient (lengthwise)		
Overturn gradient (crosswise)		35°
Turning radius		

LIGHT PONTOON CARRIER
l. Pont. Wg. (Pf. 15)

German nomenclature: leichter Pontonwagen (Pf. 15).

English designation: Light pontoon carrier (trailer).

Net weight	1,700 kg	3,747 lb.
Pay load	3,000 kg	6,614 lb.
Gross weight	4,700 kg	10,361 lb.
Weight: Front axle	2,350 kg	5,181 lb.
Weight: Rear axle	2,350 kg	5,181 lb.
Length (overall)	9,000 mm	29 ft., 6 ins.
Width (overall)	2,010 mm	6 ft., 7 ins.
Height (overall)	2,040 mm	6 ft., 8 ins.
Ground clearance	330 mm	13 ins.
Tread centers	1,700 mm	5 ft., 7 ins.
Wheelbase	4,000 mm	157 ins.
Wheel width	215 mm	8½ ins.
Angle of approach		28°
Angle of departure		25°
Seating capacity		
Fording depth		
Overturn gradient (lengthwise)		
Overturn gradient (crosswise)		35°
Turning radius		

ONTOON CARRIER
ont. Wg. (Pf. 9)

Net weight	1,378 kg	3,037 lb.
Pay load	1,774 kg	3,910 lb.
Gross weight	3,152 kg	6,947 lb.
Weight: Front axle	1,571 kg	3,464 lb.
Weight: Rear axle	1,581 kg	3,486 lb.
Length (overall)	9,050 mm	29 ft., 8 ins.
Width (overall)	1,960 mm	6 ft., 5 ins.
Height (overall)	2,240 mm	7 ft., 4 ins.
Ground clearance	400 mm	15¾ ins.
Tread centers	1,530 mm	5 ft.
Wheelbase	3,510 mm	138 ins.
Wheel width	165 mm	6½ ins.
Angle of approach		32°
Angle of departure		34°
Fording depth		
Overturn gradient (lengthwise)		
Overturn gradient (crosswise)		32°
Turning radius		

rman nomenclature: Pontonwagen (Pf. 9).

glish designation: Pontoon carrier (trailer or semi-trailer).

ONTOON CARRIER
nt. Wg. (Pf. 11)

Net weight	1,900 kg	4,188 lb.
Pay load	3,200 kg	7,055 lb.
Gross weight	5,100 kg	11,243 lb.
Weight: Front axle	2,260 kg	4,982 lb.
Weight: Rear axle	2,840 kg	6,261 lb.
Length (overall)	9,250 mm	30 ft., 4 ins.
Width (overall)	2,150 mm	7 ft.
Height (overall)	2,120 mm	6 ft., 11 ins.
Ground clearance	350 mm	13¾ ins.
Tread centers	1,610 mm	5 ft., 3 ins.
Wheelbase	3,615 mm	142 ins.
Wheel width	370 mm	14½ ins.
Angle of approach		30°
Angle of departure		25°
Fording depth		
Overturn gradient (lengthwise)		
Overturn gradient (crosswise)		
Turning radius		

rman nomenclature: Pontonwagen (Pf. 11).

glish designation: Pontoon carrier (trailer).

SOUND EQUIPMENT TRAILER
V. Gatt. fahrbar

German nomenclature: Vollgatter, fahrbar.

English designation: Sound equipment trailer.

Net weight	1,750 kg	3,857 lb.
Pay load	3,550 kg	7,826 lb.
Gross weight	5,300 kg	11,683 lb.
Weight: Front axle	2,500 kg	5,512 lb.
Weight: Rear axle	2,800 kg	6,173 lb.
Length (overall)	6,850 mm	22 ft., 5 ins.
Width (overall)	1,750 mm	5 ft., 5 ins.
Angle of approach		
Angle of departure		60°
Fording depth		
Overturn gradient (lengthwise)		
Overturn gradient (crosswise)		
Turning radius		

BRIDGING WAGON
Ramp. Wg. (Pf. 12)

German nomenclature: Rampenwagen (Pf. 12).

English designation: Bridging wagon (trailer)

Net weight	1,900 kg	4,188 lb.
Pay load	3,700 kg	8,157 lb.
Gross weight	5,600 kg	12,345 lb.
Weight: Front axle	2,500 kg	5,512 lb.
Weight: Rear axle	3,100 kg	6,834 lb.
Length (overall)	8,700 mm	28 ft., 6 ins.
Width (overall)	2,150 mm	7 ft.
Height (overall)	1,720 mm	5 ft., 8 ins.
Ground clearance	350 mm	13¾ ins.
Tread centers	1,610 mm	5 ft., 3 ins.
Wheelbase	3,615 mm	142 ins.
Wheel width	370 mm	14½ ins.
Angle of approach		30°
Angle of departure		28°
Fording depth		
Overturn gradient (lengthwise)		
Overturn gradient (crosswise)		
Turning radius		

TRAILER
efld. Anh. (o)

Net weight	5,600 kg	12,345 lb.
Pay load	20,000 kg	44,090 lb.
Gross weight	25,600 kg	56,223 lb.
Weight: Front axle	8,000 kg	17,636 lb.
Weight: Rear axle	8,800 kg	19,400 lb.
Length (overall)	8,400 mm	27 ft., 6 ins.
Width (overall)	2,750 mm	9 ft.
Height (overall)	3,000 mm	9 ft., 10 ins.
Ground clearance	270 mm	10½ ins.
Tread centers	1,720 mm	5 ft., 8 ins.
	1,900 mm	6 ft., 3 ins.
	1,900 mm	6 ft., 3 ins.
Wheelbase	3,400/1,000 mm	134/39 ins.
Wheel width	200 mm	8¼ ins.
Angle of approach		55°
Angle of departure		70°
Seating capacity		1
Fording depth		
Overturn gradient (lengthwise)		
Overturn gradient (crosswise)		
Turning radius		

German nomenclature: Tiefladeanhänger (o).

English designation: Trailer for low loads (standard commercial vehicle).

TANK TRANSPORTER
efld. Anh. f. Pz. Kpfw. (Sd. Ah. 115)

Net weight	5,000 kg	11,023 lb.
Pay load	10,000 kg	22,037 lb.
Gross weight	15,000 kg	33,060 lb.
Weight: Front axle	7,500 kg	16,534 lb.
Weight: Rear axle	7,450 kg	16,424 lb.
Length (overall)	9,680 mm	31 ft., 10 ins.
Width (overall)	2,450 mm	8 ft.
Height (overall)	1,450 mm	4 ft., 9 ins.
Ground clearance	360 mm	14½ ins.
Wheelbase	6,550 mm	256 ins.
Wheel width	480 mm	18⅞ ins.
Angle of approach		70°
Angle of departure		45°
Seating capacity		
Fording depth		
Overturn gradient (lengthwise)		
Overturn gradient (crosswise)		
Turning radius		

German nomenclature: Tiefladeanhänger fur Panzerkampfwagen (Sd. Ah. 115).

English designation: Tank transporter (heavy load trailer).

TANK TRANSPORTER

Tiefld. Anh. f. Pz. Kpfw. (Bs. Ah. 642)

German nomenclature: Tiefladeanhänger für Panzerkampfwagen (Bs. Ah. 642).

English designation: Tank transporter (heavy load
trailer).

Net weight	12,000 kg	26,450 lb.
Pay load	20,000 kg	44,090 lb.
Gross weight	32,000 kg	70,550 lb.
Weight: Front axle	8,000 kg	17,636 lb.
Weight: Rear axle	8,000 kg	17,636 lb.
Length (overall)	13,900 mm	45 ft., 7 ins.
Width (overall)	2,990 mm	9 ft., 10 ins.
Height (overall)	2,450 mm	8 ft.
Ground clearance	570 mm	22½ ins.
Tread centers	2,440 mm	8 ins.
	2,440 mm	8 ins.
	2,440 mm	8 ins.
	2,440 mm	8 ins.
Wheelbase	13/50/7,400/ 1,350 mm	53/291/53 ins.
Wheel width	480 mm	18⅞ ins.
Angle of approach		45°
Angle of departure		50°
Seating capacity		1
Fording depth		
Overturn gradient (lengthwise)		
Overturn gradient (crosswise)		
Turning radius		
WINCHES		
Hauling capacity	3,000 kg	6,614 lb.
Cable length	50 mm	164 ft.

WINCH TRAILER

Scheib. Zg. Anh.

German nomenclature: Scheibenzuganhänger mit 3
Stufen-Trommel.

English designation: Winch trailer with three drums.

Net weight	5,920 kg	13,051 lb.
Weight: Front axle	2,725 kg	6,007 lb.
Weight: Rear axle	3,195 kg	7,043 lb.
Length (overall)	6,300 mm	20 ft., 8 ins.
Width (overall)	1,980 mm	6 ft., 6 ins.
Height (overall)	2,020 mm	6 ft., 7 ins.
Ground clearance	320 mm	12⅝ ins.
Tread centers	1,520 mm	5 ft.
Wheelbase	2,930 mm	115 ins.
Wheel width	235 mm	9¼ ins.
Angle of approach		60°
Angle of departure		45°
Fording depth		
Overturn gradient (lengthwise)		90°
Overturn gradient (crosswise)		32°–40°
Turning radius		
BLOCK & TACKLE		
No. of pulleys		4
Cable length		3,000 m each
Hauling speed	5–25 km per hour	3.1–15.5 m.p.h.

NOW PLOW
Schn. Pfl. Thp. K

Net weight	400 kg	882 lb.
Length (overall)	3,100 mm	10 ft., 2 ins.
Width (overall)	2,600 mm	8 ft., 6 ins.
Height (overall)		
Ground clearance		
Angle of approach		
Angle of departure		
SNOW PLOW		
Clearing width	2.6 m	8 ft., 6 ins.
Clearing height	1.00 m	3 ft., 3 ins.

erman nomenclature: leichter Schneepflug Thp. K.

nglish designation: Snow plow.

IGHT SNOW PLOW
Schn. Pfl. Thp. E

Net weight	580 kg	1,279 lb.
Length (overall)	3,100 mm	10 ft., 2 ins.
Width (overall)	2,600 mm	8 ft., 6 ins.
Height (overall)		
Ground clearance		
Angle of approach		
Angle of departure		
SNOW PLOW		
Clearing width	2.60 m	8 ft., 6 ins.
Clearing height	1.00 m	3 ft., 3 ins.

erman nomenclature: leichter Schneepflug Thp. E.

nglish designation: Light snow plow.

MEDIUM SNOW PLOW
m. Schn. Pfl. Thp. K

Net weight	620 kg	1,356 lb.
Length (overall)	2,200 mm	7 ft., 3 ins.
Width (overall)	2,600 mm	8 ft., 6 ins.
Height (overall)	1,200 mm	3 ft., 11 ins.
Ground clearance		
Angle of approach		
Angle of departure		
SNOW PLOW		
Clearing width	2.6 m	8 ft., 6 ins.
Clearing height	1.2 m	3 ft., 3 ins.

German nomenclature: mittlerer Schneepflug Thp. K.

English designation: Medium snow plow.

MEDIUM SNOW PLOW
m. Schn. Pflg. Thp. E

Net weight	680 kg	1,500 lb.
Length (overall)	3,540 mm	11 ft., 7 ins.
Width (overall)	3,000 mm	9 ft., 10 ins.
Height (overall)	1,000 mm	3 ft., 3 ins.
Ground clearance		
Tread centers		
Wheelbase		
Angle of approach		
Angle of departure		
SNOW PLOW		
Clearing width	3.0 m	9 ft., 10 ins.
Clearing height	1.2 m	3 ft., 11 ins.

German nomenclature: schwerer Schneepflug Thp. E.

English designation: Medium snow plow.

HEAVY SNOW PLOW
Schn. Pflg. Thp. K

Net weight	980 kg	2,160 lb.
Length (overall)	2,850 mm	9 ft., 4 ins.
Width (overall)	3,000 mm	9 ft., 10 ins.
Height (overall)	1,300 mm	4 ft., 3 ins.
Ground clearance		
Angle of approach		
Angle of departure		
SNOW PLOW		
Clearing width	3.00 m	9 ft., 10 ins.
Clearing height	to 1.5 m	4 ft., 11 ins.

German nomenclature: schwerer Schneepflug Thp. K.

English designation: Heavy snow plow.

HEAVY SNOW PLOW
Schn. Pflg. Thp. E

Net weight	980 kg	2,160 lb.
Length (overall)	4,000 mm	13 ft., 1 in.
Width (overall)	2,500 mm	11 ft., 6 ins.
Height (overall)	1,200 mm	3 ft., 11 ins.
Ground clearance		
Angle of approach		
Angle of departure		
SNOW PLOW		
Clearing width	3.5 m	11 ft., 6 ins.
Clearing height	to 1.5 m	4 ft., 11 ins.

German nomenclature: schwerer Schneepflug Thp. E.

English designation: Heavy snow plow.

The famous NSU Kettenrad tractor, designated Kleine Kettenkraftrad (Sd Kfz 2), performed well in sand and mud – hence t.
popularity of this vehicle on the Russian front where this one is shown in typical conditions.

MOTOR CYCLES, SCHELL-PROGRAMM
VEHICLES AND MAULTIERS

Note: To make best use of available space only basic data is given in this section, together with relevant notes on simil
vehicles.

Mittlerer Kraftrad (o)

Medium motorcycle (commercial)

Wheelbase	1355 mm
Length (overall)	2100 mm
Height (overall)	
Width (overall)	
Tread centres	
Net weight	171 kg
Payload	
Ground clearance	
Fuel consumption	3.5L/100 km
Engine horsepower	
Piston displacement	346 cu cm
Fuel tank capacity	14 litres

Model shown – DKW NZ350

Leichter Kraftrad (o)

Light motorcycle (commercial)

Wheelbase	1230 mm
Length (overall)	1960 mm
Height (overall)	
Width (overall)	
Tread centres	
Net weight	72 kg
Payload	
Ground clearance	
Fuel consumption	2.251/100 km
Engine horsepower	
Piston displacement	123 cc
Fuel tank capacity	7.5 litres

Model shown – DKW RT125

Schwerer Kraftrad mit Beiwagenradantrieb (E)

Heavy motorcycle with side-car drive (standard)

Wheelbase	1444 mm
Length (overall)	2400 mm
Height (overall)	
Width (overall)	1730 mm
Tread centres	1180 mm
Net weight	400 kg
Payload	
Ground clearance	
Fuel consumption	6.71/100 km
Engine horsepower	
Piston displacement	745 cc
Fuel tank capacity	24 litres

Model shown – BMW R75

Schwerer Kraftrad mit Beiwagenradantrieb (E)

Heavy motorcycle with side-car drive (standard)

Wheelbase	1410 mm
Length (overall)	2385 mm
Height (overall)	1010 mm
Width (overall)	1650 mm
Tread centres	
Net weight	400 kg
Payload	
Ground clearance	
Fuel consumption	
Engine horsepower	26
Piston displacement	751 cc
Fuel tank capacity	

Model shown – Zundapp KS750

Kleines Kettenkraftrad (Sd Kfz 2)

Small tracked tractor (Special vehicle No. 2)

Length (overall)	3000 mm
Height (overall)	1200 mm
Width (overall)	1000 mm
Tread centres	
Net weight	1235 kg
Payload	
Ground clearance	
Fuel consumption .16l/100km	
Engine horsepower	36
Piston displacement	1478 cc
Fuel tank capacity	42 litres
Model – NSU HK101	

Standard vehicle shown above; below are shown two special purpose types (data as for standard vehicle except different height and weight).

LEFT: **Kleines Kettenkraftrad fru Feldfernkabel (Sd Kfz 2/1)** – small tracked tractor for field telephone cable.

RIGHT: **Kleines Kettenkraftrad fur schweres Feldkabel (Sd Kfz 2/2)** – small tracked tractor for heavy field cable.

Leichter Personenkraftwagen (Sfz 1) mit Fahrgestell des le Pkw K1 Typ 82

Light personnel carrier on the chassis of the light car Typ 82

Wheelbase	2400
Length (overall)	3740 mm
Height (overall)	1650 mm
Width (overall)	1600 mm
Tread centres	1356/1360 mm
Net weight	685 kg
Payload	
Ground clearance	290 mm
Fuel consumption	
Engine horsepower	24
Piston displacement	985/1131 cc*
Fuel tank capacity	40 litres

* Later models

Schell-Programm Light Cars

BELOW: Standard model of le Pkw Ki Typ 82 (Volkswagen Typ 82). Vehicle could also be fitted as an ambulance or engineer truck.

Fernsprechkraftwagen (Sfz 2)

telephone car

Funkkraftwagen (Sfz 2)

Radio car

Leichter Messtruppkraftwagen (Sfz 3)

Light survey section car

leichter Personenkraftwagen (Kfz 1/20) gl/wg Schwimmifahiger Gelandeng Typ 166

Light personnel carrier on chassis of cross-country amphibious vehicle Type 166

Wheelbase	2000 mm
Length (overall)	3825 mm
Height (overall)	1615 mm
Width (overall)	1480 mm
Tread centres	2000 mm
Net weight	890 kg
Payload	
Ground clearance	265 mm
Fuel consumption	
Engine horsepower	24
Piston displacement	985/1131 cc*
Fuel tank capacity	50 litres

*Later models

Similar in concept to the VW Schwimmwagen, but heavier and with four-wheel drive, the Trippel SG38 (and later but similar models) saw limited military service but was not adopted as a standard type.

Schell-Programm Trucks

Krankenkraftwagen Kfz 31 l.gl. Lkw. A-Typ

Ambulance (Typ 31) on light cross-country truck, A-Type

Wheelbase	3270 mm
Length (overall)	5200 mm
Height (overall)	2085 mm
Width (overall)	1980 mm
Tread centres	1535/1618 mm
Net weight	3000 kg
Payload	
Ground clearance	
Fuel consumption	
Engine horsepower	50
Piston displacement	2678 cc
Fuel tank capacity	72 litres

Model shown – Phanomen-Granit 1500A (right).
N.B. Einheitskastenaufbau – standard box body – as shown was also used in other roles, eg. radio truck, repair truck)

Kommandeurwagen (Kfz 21) mit Fahrgestell des le Lkw A-Typ

Command car (Type 21) on chassis of light truck, Type A.

Wheelbase	3250 mm
Length (overall)	5080 mm
Height (overall)	2100 mm
Width (overall)	1850 mm
Tread centres	
Net weight	
Payload	
Ground clearance	
Fuel consumption	30l/100 km
Engine horsepower	85
Piston displacement	3517 cc
Fuel tank capacity	120 litres

Model shown — Steyr 1500A/01

Fernsprech/kraftwagen (Kfz 15) mit Fahrgestell des le Lkw A-Typ

Telephone truck (Type 15) on chassis of light truck Type A

Wheelbase	3250 mm
Length (overall)	5080 mm
Height (overall)	2320 mm
Width (overall)	2000 mm
Tread centres	
Net weight	2485 kg
Payload	
Ground clearance	
Fuel consumption	30l/100 km
Engine horsepower	85
Piston displacement	3517 cc
Fuel tank capacity	120 litres

Model shown — Steyr 1500A/02

Two typical Typ-S 3 tonners are shown. Borgward, Daimler-Benz (see chassis, page 14) and Magirus were other major builders of this type.

The three most common bodies fitted to the 1.5 ton A-Typ 4 × chassis are shown here. Both the Mannschaftswagen body (abov and the Einheitskastenaufbau box body (previous page) were us for many different roles. One further body in wide use was the car truck type. Daimler-Benz were the other main builder of the 1.5 t A-Typ chassis.

Mittlerer Lastkraftwagen Offen (S-Typ)

Medium open truck Type S

Wheelbase	4013 m
Length (overall)	6390 m
Height (overall)	2175 m
Width (overall)	2250 m
Tread centres	
Net weight	2540
Payload	3 ton
Ground clearance	
Fuel consumption	
Engine horsepower	
Piston displacement	
Fuel tank capacity	

Model shown — Ford V3000S

Mittlerer Laskraftwagen Offen (o)/(S-Typ)

Medium open truck (o) Type S

Wheelbase	3600 m
Length (overall)	6700 m
Height (overall)	2300 m
Width (overall)	2265 m
Tread centres	1542/1620 m
Net weight	3000 kg (appr
Payload	3 ton
Ground clearance	220 m
Fuel consumption	
Engine horsepower	
Piston displacement	3626
Fuel tank capacity	92 lit

Model shown — Opel 3.6-36 Typ-S

The ordnance designation Kfz 305 was given to vehicles with the standard body, with a suffix to indicate the individual role. For example Funkraftwagen carried the designations Kfz 305/16 to Kfz 305/20 dependent on function. These vehicles were intended to replace the specialist vehicles with different types of body shown earlier in this book.

Mittlerer Scheinwerferkraftwagen mit Fahrgestell des S Lkw (A-Typ)

Medium searchlight truck on chassis of Type A heavy truck

Wheelbase	4875 mm
Length (overall)	8050 mm
Height (overall)	2725 mm
Width (overall)	2370 mm
Tread centres	1980/1765 mm
Net weight	6250 kg
Payload	4½ tonne
Ground clearance	
Fuel consumption	24.51/100 km
Engine horsepower	105
Piston displacement	7412 cc
Fuel tank capacity	120 litres
Model shown − Bussing-NAG 4.500A	

Note: Special purpose vehicle illustrated; the standard cargo truck, schweres gelandegangiger Lastkraftwagen (A-Typ) − heavy cross-country Type A truck − was externally similar.

Schwerer Lastkraftwagen mit geschlossenem Ginheitsaufbau (A-Typ)

Heavy truck, Type A, with standard house body

Wheelbase	4875 mm
Length (overall)	8050 mm
Height (overall)	2725 mm
Width (overall)	2370 mm
Tread centres	1980/1765 mm
Net weight	6250 kg
Payload	
Ground clearance	

Lastkraftwagen (3t) mit geschlossenem Aufban (Kfz 305)

3 ton truck with box-van body (Type 305)

Wheelbase	3600 mm
Length (overall)	6700 mm
Height (overall)	2860 mm
Width (overall)	2265 mm
Tread centres	1542/1620 mm
Net weight	3500 kg (approx)
Payload	
Ground clearance	22 mm
Fuel consumption	
Engine horsepower	75
Piston displacement	3626 cc
Fuel tank capacity	92 litres
Model shown − Opel 3.6 36 Typ-S	

Funkkraftwagen Au.B mit Fahrgestell des m Lkw (A-Typ)

Radio truck type A or B on chassis of Type A medium truck

Wheelbase	3450 mm
Length (overall)	6300 mm
Height (overall)	2895 mm
Width (overall)	2120 mm
Tread centres	1630/1642 mm
Net weight	3250 kg
Payload	
Ground clearance	25 mm
Fuel consumption	
Engine horsepower	75
Piston displacement	3626 cc
Fuel tank capacity	92 litres
Model shown − Opel 3.6-6700A	

Fuel consumption	24.51/100 km
Engine horsepower	105
Piston displacement	7412 cc
Fuel tank capacity	120 litres
Model shown − Bussing-NAG 4.500A	

Note: As with the 3 ton class the Einheitskastenaufbau body in the 4½ ton class suited the vehicle for employment in many roles − radio van, oxygen charging, workshop, etc. The Bussing-NAG 4.500S (4 × 2) chassis (see page 15) was also used with the Einheitskastenaufbau. MAN and Daimler-Benz 4½ ton class chassis were also used with this body.

Schwerer gelandegangiger Lastkraft-wagen, offen (A-Typ)

Heavy cross-country open truck, Type A

Wheelbase	4785 mm
Length (overall)	8550 mm
Height (overall)	3100 mm
Width (overall)	2500 mm
Tread centres	
Net weight	8350 kg
Payload	6½ tonne
Ground clearance	
Fuel consumption	
Engine horsepower	210
Piston displacement	14825 cc
Fuel tank capacity	
Model shown – Tatra 6500A III	▶

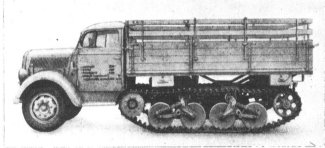

Gleiskettenlastkraftwagen 4½t, offen (Maultier)

Tracked truck, 4½ ton, open (Maultier)

Wheelbase	
Length (overall)	7900 mm
Height (overall)	3350mm
Width (overall)	2350 mm
Tread centres	
Net weight	6000 kg (approx)
Payload	4½ tonne
Ground clearance	
Fuel consumption	
Engine horsepower	112
Piston displacement	7274 cc
Fuel tank capacity	
Model shown – Daimler-Benz L4500R	

Note: Both the vehicle illustrated here and the Tatra 6500A III shown at top of pace carry the Einheitsfahrerhaus, utility 'ersatz' cab which could be seen fitted to any Schell-Programm truck built from 1944 onwards. ▶

Maultier Trucks

Gleiskettenlastkraftwagen 2t, offen (Maultier) (Sd Kfz 3)

Tracked truck, 2 ton, open (Maultier) (Special type

Wheelbase	
Length (overall)	6120
Height (overall)	2800
Width (overall)	2220
Tread centres	
Net weight	465C
Payload	2 to
Ground clearance	
Fuel consumption	
Engine horsepower	
Piston displacement	
Fuel tank capacity	
Model shown – Klockner-Humboldt-Dentz S.3000/SSM	

Note: Chassis shown on page 14.

Gleiskettenlastkraftwagen 2t, offen (Maultier) (Sd Kfz 3)

Tracked truck, 2 ton, open (Maultier) (Special type

Wheelbase	
Length (overall)	6000
Height (overall)	2710
Width (overall)	2280
Tread centres	
Net weight	393C
Payload	2 to
Ground clearance	22
Fuel consumption	
Engine horsepower	
Piston displacement	362€
Fuel tank capacity	82 li
Model shown – Opel 3.6 – 36S/SSM	

Note: Ford chassis was also used for Maultier conversion – se picture on page 14.

RACTORS

...ditions on the Eastern front where roads already poor were
...ed to seas of mud or slush in winter, dictated the development
...e Raupenschleppe-Ost (tracked tractor-east) as a load carrier and
...ing vehicle. Built by Steyr, the original model (RSO/01) had a
...mercial type pressed steel truck cab and wood cargo body. The
...or production model, however (RSO/03) had a much simplified
...with flat panels and folding canvas top. These RSOs proved very
...ul and some were later used on the Western front in 1945.
...ugh not wheeled in the sense of a truck, these vehicles are
...ded in this book since they were mainly intended to fulfil the role
...truck. Czech-built Praga tractors, also included in this book, saw
...e extensive service mainly for towing artillery or carrying
...nunition. Major wheeled artillery tractors were the Hanomag
...00 Schwerer Radschlepper (shown on this page) and a very
...lar Faun vehicle. A heavy 6 × 6 tractor built by Kaeble saw
...ed service to tow heavy trailers and ordnance. For service in
...sia the Ostradschlepper (east wheeled tractor) was produced,
... large spudded wheels and conventional truck cab and body.
...se vehicles were built by Skoda and designed by Dr Porsche, the
...designer. The various smaller tractors shown in this book were
...ly used by the Luftwaffe for towing aircraft and trailers on
...elds.

...upenschlepper-Ost

...cked tractor — east

...eelbase	
...gth (overall)	4425 mm
...ht (overall)	2520 mm
...th (overall)	1990 mm
...d centres	
...weight..	3500 kg
...oad	1500 kg
...ind clearance	
...consumption	
...ne horsepower......................................	70
...on displacement	3517 cc
...tank capacity.......................................	

...els shown — Steyr RSO/01 (upper) and Steyr RSO/03 (lower)

...t-Radschlepper

...t wheeled tractor

...elbase...	3000 mm
...th (overall)	5475 mm
...ht (overall)	2780 mm
...:h (overall)	2300 mm
...d centres	
...weight..	
...oad...	
...ind clearance	
...consumption.......................................	
...ne horsepower....................................	80
...on displacement	
...tank capacity.......................................	

...el shown — Skoda 175

TRAILERS

A big selection of trailers is shown in this book, most of them having
a clearly defined function. It is worth pointing out that the various
Sonderhanger (special trailers) shown were considered to be
transport items, not part of the artillery equipment (eg, Flak 36) to
which they were normally fitted.

Late in the war the appearance of very heavy tanks necessitated
the procurement of heavy commercial trailers and examples of these
are shown. Even these were too narrow to carry a Tiger or King Tiger
tank properly and the tracks of these vehicles overhung the trailer
sides.

In the latter half of the war larger trailers were taken into service to
accommodate heavier tanks. Tiefladeanhanger fur PzKpfw (Bs Ah
116) (LEFT) was an uprated version of Ah 642 (page 116). Gross
weight 35800 kg, payload 23000 kg. Gotha 60 tonne (BOTTOM
LEFT) and 68 tonne were commercial trailers used to carry Panther
and Tiger tanks.

Appendix 1

The following listing identifies by page (number) and position (upper, first) most of the vehicle chassis illustrated between pages 17–70. Where positive identification is not possible the name is omitted.

17. Opel Kadett, BMW 303
18. Stoewer 40, BMW 303
19. Stoewer 40, Horch 830BI
20. Opel P4, Stoewer 40
21. Horch 830BI, BMW 303
22. Hanomag ZOB, BMW 325
23. Horch 830BI, Stoewer 40
24. – Horch 830
25. Wanderer W11, Daimler-Benz 320
26. Horch EFm, Horch 830
27. Horch EFm, Opel EFm
28. Daimler-Benz 340, Horch EFm
29. Opel EFm, Horch 830BI
30. Opel EFm, Opel EFm
31. Opel EFm, Daimler-Benz 200
32. Daimler-Benz, Horch V8
33. Horch EFm, Horch EFm 1a
34. Horch EFm 1a, Krupp L2H 143
35. Horch EFm, Krupp L2H 143
36. Horch EFm 1a, Phanomen-Granit
37. Horch EFm, Krupp L2H 143
38. Horch EFm, Krupp L2H 143
39. Horch EFm, Krupp L2H 143
40. Horch EFm, Krupp L2H 143
41. Phanomen-Granit, Daimler-Benz G3a
42. Einheitsdiesel, Einheitsdiesel
43. Daimler-Benz G3a, Bussing-NAG G31
44. Einheitsdiesel, Daimler-Benz G3a
45. Magirus M206, Einheitsdiesel
46. Magirus M206, Einheitsdiesel
47. Magirus M206, Einheitsdiesel

48. Bussing-NAG G31, Einheitsdiesel
49. Daimler-Benz G3a, Daimler-Benz G3a
50. Daimler-Benz G3a, Daimler-Benz G3a
51. Daimler-Benz G3a, Daimler-Benz G3a
52. Daimler-Benz G3a, Einheitsdiesel
53. Daimler-Benz G3a, Opel 3.6–36S
54. Daimler-Benz G3a, Bussing-NAG 650
55. Daimler-Benz G3a, Henschel 33G1
56. Krupp L3H63, Krupp L3H63
57. Henschel 33G1, Krupp L3H63
58. Krupp, L3H63, Henschel 33G1
59. Henschel 33G1, Krupp L3H163
60. Daimler-Benz LG3000, Krupp L3H163
61. Bussing-NAG III GL6, Bussing-NAG III GL6
62. Daimler-Benz LG3000, Bussing-NAG commercial
63. , Henschel
64. Henschel, Daimler-Benz
65. , Bussing-NAG III GL6
67. Henschel L3H163,
68. Opel 3.6–36S, Henschel.
69.   Henschel 33G1

Appendix 2

VEHICLE builders' trade-marks, which were usually displayed on most new vehicles, are shown right. The following makes of tyres were fitted on German wheeled military vehicles. Dunlop, Fulda, Metzeller, Semperit, Deka, Continental, and Phoenix.

ADLER	AUTO-UNION	BORGWARD
HANOMAG	HENSCHEL	KRUPP
MAGIRUS	MAYBACH	MERCEDES-BENZ